THE 10% SHIFT

Design: Mark Pate

ISBN: 979-8-234-00134-4

Printed in the United States of America

Kate Moynihan

THE 10% SHIFT

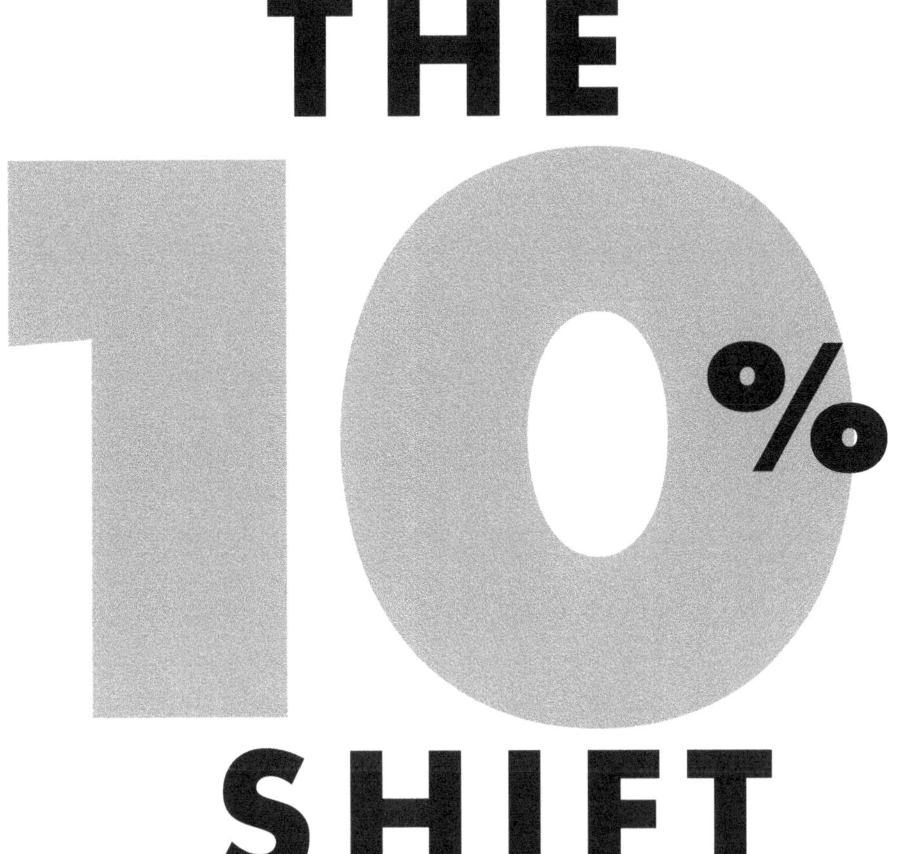

Small Resets.
Gentle Forward Motion.
The Magic of Rediscovery.

Author's Note

This book grew out of lived experience, not theory.

What you will find here are stories and reflections shaped by real moments—times when life felt uncertain, tender, or quietly demanding a change. I didn't write this book to offer answers or prescriptions. I wrote it as a companion for anyone standing in a season of transition, sensing a quiet need for something to shift, but not knowing how—or how much.

The 10% Shift is not a memoir. It's a guide born from experience—written for people who want to move forward without forcing, rushing, or reinventing themselves from scratch. It's for those who believe that small, intentional choices can gently change the direction of a life.

You don't need to know my whole story to use what's here.

You only need to be willing to notice what feels true for you.

Take what resonates.

Move at your own pace.

Let the rest fall away.

And if you find yourself reading a chapter from the hot tub, spoon in hand, devouring the entire pint of Ben & Jerry's Coffee Heath ice cream, know that you're in very good company.

With heart,
Kate

How These Stories Move

The stories in this book aren't told in chronological order.

They're arranged by insight, not age.

They move across seasons of life—circling back, deepening, and returning—much the way understanding does.

• Younger years — early identity, belonging, first brave choices

• Early adulthood — motherhood & loss

• Midlife — relocation, reinvention, returning to school

• Later midlife — partnership, creative work, steadiness

You don't need to keep track of when everything happened.

Only notice what resonates now.

If it helps, keep a notebook/journal nearby as you read—not to analyze or capture everything, but to jot down what quietly stirs or returns. Sometimes a single sentence is enough.

Table of Contents

Introduction

Small Shifts, Steady Ground

Most of us don't arrive at change because we're inspired.

We arrive because something has loosened.

A certainty. A role.

A version of ourselves we thought would hold.

Sometimes that unraveling looks dramatic.

And sometimes it looks like melting into a bubble bath, hiding from your own thoughts, devouring the entire bag of Australian black licorice, wondering how you got here.

If you've been there, you're not alone.

For a long time, I believed change required courage in large quantities—dramatic decisions, bold declarations, the kind of bravery that looks good from the outside.

What I've learned instead is quieter and far more sustainable: Meaningful change often begins with small shifts. Subtle adjustments in how we listen, how we respond, how we stay present when we'd rather escape.

This book isn't about reinvention. It's about return.

Return to your inner compass.

Return to what steadies you.

Return to the part of you that already knows how to move forward—gently, imperfectly, and with self-trust.

The stories in these pages move across decades, not to document a life in chronological order, but to illuminate moments of learning. Times when I resisted change. Times when I rushed it. And times when I finally allowed myself to take the smallest possible step and discovered it was enough.

There is a marriage before this life and a love that comes after it.

I don't unpack that first ending here—not because it didn't matter, but because this book is about what we do *after* the ground gives way.

What matters for this story is this: Loss did not end my capacity to love. It deepened it.

That truth sits beneath everything that follows.

The 10% Shift is an invitation—not to fix your life, but to tend to it. To notice where you're gripping too tightly. To recognize when your nervous system needs steadiness more than answers. To trust that forward motion doesn't require clarity about the whole path—only willingness to take the next small step.

You won't find prescriptions here. You won't be asked to overhaul who you are.

Instead, you'll be offered reflections, stories, and practices meant to help you recalibrate—again and again—when life turns uncertain, or loud, or unexpectedly quiet.

If you're reading this, something may already be shifting.

You don't need to rush it.

You don't need to name it yet.

You only need to begin where you are.

PART I
BEGIN AGAIN

Chapter One
What Is a Restart?

Restarts repeat long before we recognize them.

That's why the stories in this chapter move between my youth, my thirties, and midlife — not to confuse you, but to show you how quietly they arrive. Restarts don't announce themselves. They slip in early, often disguised as negotiation, compromise, or practicality.

For me, one of the first looked like this:

- staying in ballet classes I hated so I could earn permission for a sleepover I was deemed "too young" for
- becoming a nurse after my high school sweetheart didn't propose
- packing up and moving to a city where no one knew my name

And yes — I did all of that.

At the time, I didn't know these were restarts.

I thought I was being responsible. Flexible. Easy to live with.

What I didn't understand yet was this: A restart isn't always a bold decision.

Sometimes it's the first moment you trade what feels acceptable for what feels true.

That's the beginning of a restart.

A small shift. Sometimes just ten percent.

The Myth of Reinvention vs. The Power of a Shift

In my early thirties, I believed that if something wasn't working, the solution was reinvention — the big, sweeping kind.

New city. New life. New you.

I moved nearly a thousand miles — from Michigan to North Dakota — believing that a fresh start, paired with the right relationship, could build the happiness I hadn't yet learned to create on my own.

It didn't.

The ending came quickly and without ceremony.

No happily ever after.

What I learned then — and would spend years fully understanding — was this: reinvention asks you to outrun yourself.

And eventually, you run out of road.

When reinvention collapses, it doesn't leave you wiser.

It leaves you tired.

That's the price tag no one mentions.

Reinvention is exhausting.

And deeply overrated.

So I began breaking change into smaller pieces.

Mini-reinventions. Micro-movements. Small resets.

My first shift came when I needed to find a place of my own in Bismarck — heartbroken, stranded, and too ashamed to return home.

With only nickels left in my checking account, I rented a cracker-box basement apartment in an aging house. Narrow windows let in only a sliver of daylight.

Under a dim lamp, I doodled. Actually — scribbled.

I was too confused to make sense of my markings.

Then came a rapid tap-tap-tap at the door.

My landlord, Marge, burst in. She took one look at my swollen eyes, slumped shoulders, and frantic lines on the paper.

"I know just the place for you," she said, grabbing my hand and whisking me off to the local college art department, where she happened to be taking a pottery class.

And standing there — in that buzzing, imperfect, alive art room — I felt it.

Energy. Possibility. Relief.

It wasn't clarity. But it was enough.

Enough to take one shaky step forward. Which led to another.

That's when I learned something essential: You don't have to up-end your life.

You just need to approach it differently.

Sometimes a restart is simply the moment you stop struggling alone and accept the help that's already reaching for you.

Emotional Weather

Before any restart, there's emotional weather.

Sunshine. Storms. Fog.

Sometimes, all in the same afternoon.

You can't change your life if you don't pay attention to the forecast inside you—the thunder in your ribcage, the lightning in your gut.

Even now, in midlife, storms still roll in unexpectedly.

Not long ago, I felt so off that even the dog seemed concerned. Nothing was technically wrong—I just felt scrambled. As if my inner forecast had shifted without warning from a calm, balmy sixty degrees to sharp sleet.

The tipping point? Soup.

Specifically, an easy shrimp corn chowder recipe I'd made a dozen times.

My eighty-year-old mom—an invited dinner guest—peered into the pot like a judge on a cooking show and announced, loudly enough for the shrimp to hear, that she had always made her soup stock from scratch.

Tension snapped, crackled, and popped—ten times louder than the Rice Krispie treats I'd made earlier.

I didn't snap. I bit my tongue.

Then five grandkids and four adults burst through the door moments later, resetting the room with hugs, noise, and laughter.

Or so I thought.

Later that night, standing alone at the sink, the truth surfaced: I was carrying things that weren't mine.

Mom's tension wasn't mine. Her worries weren't mine. Her habits weren't mine.

And I could put them down.

That was a restart. Quiet. Mighty.

When emotional weather becomes emotional clarity, change becomes possible.

So... What Is a Restart?

After decades of loving, losing myself, finding myself, and nearly unraveling over soup, here's my definition:

A restart is the moment you choose to live more honestly, more authentically, and more gently as yourself.

It's not a makeover. It's alignment.

A restart can look like:

- asking for help before you hit the wall
- letting go of what doesn't belong to you
- saying no using one sentence—or even one word
- trading rigid rules for flexibility while staying true to your happiness
- laughing at yourself instead of shaming yourself

Restarts are often tiny.

Invisible to everyone else.

But inside? They're enormous.

Small shifts move big mountains. Sometimes all it takes is ten percent.

Your First Step

You don't need to overhaul your life. You don't need to reinvent yourself. You don't need a five-year plan.

You just need to notice: Your emotional weather. Your whispers. Your nudges.

Attention is the first step. Compassion is the second. Everything else unfolds gently from there.

And here you are—reading, breathing, curious.

Which tells me something important: You've already begun your restart.

Chapter Two
The 10% Shift

Why Small Changes Stick, Soften, and Save Your Sanity

If someone had told me the secret to changing my life wasn't a spreadsheet, a revelation, or a cross-country escape—but a 10% shift—I would've said, "Wonderful. Which ten percent? Because ninety percent of this circus is still jumping through rings of fire."

Many of us don't need permission to make big, dramatic changes.

What we often need is permission to make the small, compassionate, internal ones.

A 10% shift isn't glamorous.

It looks like choosing calm.

Listening before explaining.

Softening instead of forcing.

A 10% shift is the smallest possible move toward yourself.

And somehow—the most powerful.

Your Closet Knows Before You Do

Here's something I noticed in my mid-twenties.

On cool mornings, overwhelmed as a mom of two toddlers, I reached for the same sweater every time—a soft blue cable-knit, its sleeves stretched from love.

The color matched the sleeveless summer shirt I'd worn all season. Which matched the faded jeans I always felt most myself in.

That's when it hit me: Most of my closet wasn't for me.

It was for an imaginary woman—the one who was the loving the homemaker role she admired in her own mother.

The one who was supposed to feel fulfilled ironing on Tuesdays, making pie crust from scratch on Wednesdays, and wearing an animal-print blouse while pushing a double-wide stroller through the subdivision.

My clothes were trying to tell me something: *Your insides want calm. Please stop dressing for approval.*

That day, I held up the blouse with the printed cheetahs and asked, "Does this feel like me—or like who I thought I was supposed to be?"

The answer came quietly. Clearly. No.

And that's when it clicked. If I could trust my closet…maybe I could trust my life.

Style and color became a gentle guide for changing my life—not a makeover, but a micro-correction.

A 10% shift.

A whisper I didn't yet know would grow louder.

The Gray Moment Shift

One of the quietest 10% shifts of my life happened on a river, in a canoe.

It was the day Larry, my husband, proposed—that part was big— but the shift inside me was small, soft, and unexpectedly steady.

It was my first time in a canoe. I was thirty-eight.

The morning began warm and tender, the kind of September light that makes you think the day has made a promise.

Then the weather changed its mind.

Cold drizzle. Gray sky. Gray water. Gray canoe.

My hair plastered to my head.

My jeans glued to my legs.

My feet—two cold bricks—anchored to the aluminum floor.

For hours, I was certain I would never choose the color gray again.

Not for a shirt. Not for a wall. Not for a single throw pillow.

And then I turned around. Larry was on one knee. In an instant, gray transformed.

Not gloomy—grounded.

Not cold—steady.

Not bleak—honest.

Ever since, gray has been my shorthand for:

- safety
- steadiness
- emotional exhale
- calm water inside myself

It didn't change my whole life.

It changed how I entered my life.

A 10% shift.

When the World Went Digital
And So Did I

Growing up in the late 1950s, *digital* meant fingers. We counted on our hands—literally.

Now it means screens, speed, and a world that rarely pauses.

I was slow to convert.

I had a landline at my art gallery. And one at home. That was enough ringing for me.

And then... I retired.

Suddenly, no one urgently needed me. And I wasn't sure what I needed, either.

My memoir, *A Lone Birch, My Artistic Journey*, had just launched. I gave a few talks. I liked guiding women.

Then the world shut down when COVID hit.

The talks paused. And I found myself in a new chapter: solo entrepreneurship – meaning just me, myself, and I.

Suddenly, I had to learn Instagram. I didn't even know it required square photos.

This chapter felt like wanting to paint a masterpiece—only to discover every tube of paint had dried solid.

Some days I thought, "I survived toddlerhood and gallery ownership. Why is this tiny app defeating me?"

Because transitions are humbling. Even the good ones.

But every small win—posting one photo without deleting the whole app, finding the alt-text box, learning how to insert an emoji —became its own 10% shift. (*Full honesty: learning how to use the right emoji felt like a very ambitious 10% shift.*)

One small click at a time, I learned:

- a new way to show up
- a new way to connect
- a new way to be me with shameless vulnerability

Not glamorous. But growth rarely is.

What 10% Actually Feels Like

Here's the truth no one tells you: A 10% shift often feels like... nothing.

It looks like:

- having a slightly kinder bedtime
- cleaning one drawer
- using the good mug
- softening your tone with yourself
- leaving one thing off your list—on purpose
- wearing the colors your soul keeps reaching for
- asking for help before you hit the meltdown threshold

(Yes—even if "help" means taking an online Instagram class from a twenty-year-old with self-tanner stripes and more confidence than gravity should legally allow.)

These changes are small. But small grows.

Your life rarely changes all at once.

It changes in increments that your nervous system can handle.

A 10% shift is compassion disguised as progress.

It asks: "What's the next gentle thing?"

Not: "What's the next impressive thing?"

Your 10% Shift (A Beginning)

You don't have to change everything.

You just have to change something.

A restart begins when you shift 10% toward the woman you're becoming.

And you wouldn't be here if something inside you wasn't already waking up.

PART II
BUILD YOUR INNER COMPASS

Chapter Three
Emotional Weather

Learning to Bend, Not Break

If you had asked me in my earlier years whether I was "resilient," I probably would've said something like, "Well... I haven't died yet, so maybe?"

Back then, I thought resilience meant toughness.

Grit-your-teeth-and-plow-through toughness.

White-knuckle-your-way-forward toughness.

Act-fine-even-when-you're-unraveling-inside toughness.

But that isn't resilience. That's performance.

Real resilience—the kind that lasts—is quieter. Gentler. Almost shy.

This chapter weaves stories from my thirties, sixties, and the years in between—because emotional weather doesn't follow a calendar. Storms arrive when they want to. So does calm.

Resilience isn't about standing rigid in the wind.

It's elasticity.

It's learning to bend without breaking.

And if you're reading this, you already know how to do that.

You just might not call it resilience yet.

The Snowmobile Lesson
There Is No Try.

It happened at a bridal retreat, of all places—after I had retired from owning the gallery.

The room was filled with bridal shop owners: women who could soothe a meltdown, pin a hem, negotiate with a mother-in-law, and calm a nervous bride before their first coffee refill.

It had been a long day for them.

And I was the final inspirational speaker—a title still new enough to make me sweat through my blouse. Could I hold their attention for ninety full minutes?

I walked in carrying my stories and a Stress Release Survival Kit for each of them, assuming they'd be ready for something interactive.

On the outside, I looked prepared.

On the inside, the gremlins were loud. *You don't belong here. Why you? Who do you think you are?*

This, I've learned, is emotional weather.

The kind that rolls in quietly—right before you're asked to show up.

The kind that tests whether you'll grip tighter… or bend.

To make matters worse, I'd saved the big reveal—the stress-release goodies—for the end, thinking it would be the perfect way to revive any nodding heads.

Even though I knew that blowing Q-tips through straws at tiny paper "Bridezillas" would eventually get them laughing, self-doubt twisted in my gut.

And that's when resilience asked me a question.

Not *Can you be perfect?*

But *Can you be honest?*

On impulse, I told them a story I hadn't planned to share.

Years earlier, my then-fiancé, Larry, had taken me snowmobiling. Keep in mind: I turn green just looking at a roller coaster.

But he charmed me into climbing on behind him. The moment he revved the engine; the machine vibrated up my spine and rattled my teeth—and not from the cold. I closed my eyes. There were no stars to wish upon anyway.

We bounced along… until we didn't.

Larry swerved to avoid a squirrel, and I launched straight into a snowdrift.

There I lay, sprawled like a snow angel who'd given up halfway.

Larry circled back, lifted his visor, and said, "Hop back on."

Inside, I wanted to walk home—through the woods, barefoot, in a blizzard—anything but getting back on that machine. But embarrassment won.

So I offered the compromise I still regret. "I'll try."

He shook his head. "There is no try. Just do."

I didn't know he was quoting Yoda. I just knew I wanted to throw a snowball at him.

But he wasn't wrong.

Resilience isn't about trying harder. It's about deciding.

- I will stand up.
- I will move forward.
- I will take the next small step—even if I'm trembling.

When I finished the story for the bridal shop owners, the room exhaled.

They knew the truth of it: Resilience isn't about being strong.

It's about being willing.

From Palette Knife to Brushstroke
Letting Go of What Worked

I painted watercolors for eighteen years before switching to oils during the 2008 recession. Ever since, the palette knife felt like an extension of my arm.

Bold. Thick. Textured.

It was the tool I trusted.

Then came an invitation that knocked me sideways: my first solo show at the Holland Area Arts Council.

There was just one catch.

"Your show needs to be different," they said. "Tell a story. Have a theme."

A theme? A story?

This wasn't a small shift. It was an internal flip—the kind that makes your stomach twist like taffy.

For nearly twenty-five years, I had worked within a rhythm that felt steady and familiar. My paintings lived in my gallery. They rotated naturally with the seasons. Tulips in spring. Fiery orange leaves in autumn. A blanket of snow in January.

I painted one piece at a time.

If a shoreline sold, I painted another.

If a birch resonated, I explored the idea a little deeper.

There was no requirement to connect the dots.

No demand for a through-line.

No pressure to explain myself.

And suddenly, I was being asked to do exactly that.

What story was I supposed to tell? What thread tied my work together? And what if I didn't have one?

That's when I remembered Picasso's eleven-bull lithograph series—how he stripped the bull down, sketch by sketch, until only the essence remained.

Could I do that with my beloved birch trees? Strip away the detail? Set aside the texture? Let go of my security blanket—the palette knife?

Self-doubt perched on one shoulder. Insecurity took the other.

Thirty pieces. For a solo show.

My eyes burned with stress sweat.

Then a thought arrived: What if I didn't just deconstruct birch trees? What if I did the same with flowers—my second love?

I saw it instantly. Fifteen birches on one wall. Fifteen blooms on the other.

I did it.

The show opened.

The accolades poured in.

And not one painting sold.

My heart cracked.

And that's when resilience whispered: Keep going. Let curiosity lead.

Resilience isn't mastery.

It's willingness.

The courage to evolve—even when the landing is hard and not softened by a snowbank.

What Birch Trees Know

I first became inspired by birch trees when I took one brave step back to college as an art major.

At the time, I was far from home—in North Dakota, where birch trees are rare and familiar landmarks disappeared.

Back in Michigan, on a camping trip with my sons, I noticed one particular birch. A small one wedged among towering oaks. It should've been swallowed by their shadows.

But it stood tall—craggy bark and all—unapologetic in its imperfections.

Remarkably, birch trees don't grow by holding on. They grow by shedding. Quietly peeling away outer layers that no longer serve them, growing stronger beneath what they release, reaching higher—reminding me to do the same.

That's resilience.

You shed. You let the new layer breathe. You grow.

None of us stays the same. We're not meant to.

Staying locked in place doesn't protect us. It stunts us.

The Real Definition of Resilience

Resilience isn't:

- being stoic
- powering through
- pretending
- pushing past your limits
- ignoring overwhelming moments

Resilience is:

- bending without breaking
- returning to your center when the time is right
- allowing change
- trusting you'll find your footing again
- being gentle with yourself while you relearn your life

It's not toughness.

It's elasticity.

You don't spring back to who you were.

You spring forward—to who you're becoming—carrying your essence with you.

Your Resilience
A Quiet Truth

If you're reading this, you've already lived through things you didn't think you could handle.

You are already resilient.

You've survived disappointments.

Navigated transitions.

Carried more than you planned.

Rebuilt routines.

Adapted again and again.

Maybe it wasn't graceful. (Worry not—none of us look graceful in a storm.)

But you moved. You shifted. You bent.

And when the emotional weather passed—as it always does—you found your way back to yourself. That's resilience.

If you want to try this on in real life, begin here: Notice one place in your life where you bent instead of broke. That noticing alone is a 10% shift.

And sometimes, the next lesson isn't how to bend—it's how to keep going when you're already carrying more than your share.

That's where resilience becomes practice.

Small Shifts, Full Hands

Not every restart happens in open space.

Some happen while you're caring for aging parents.

Or raising children who still need you.

Or supporting a partner through illness, change, or uncertainty.

Or managing work deadlines, financial pressure, and the quiet weight of being the one who holds everything together.

If that's you, hear this clearly: You are not behind. You are not doing it wrong.

And you are not asking for too much by wanting something to shift.

There are seasons when you cannot drop the load. You cannot step away. You cannot make bold changes without consequences for others.

That doesn't mean change isn't possible. It means it must be gentler.

A 10% shift doesn't require more time, more energy, or a dramatic exit. It asks for honesty—often just with yourself.

Sometimes the shift is internal: releasing guilt as a motivator, letting go of the belief that caring for others means disappearing.

Sometimes the shift is practical:

- asking for help without a speech
- saying no to one small thing
- allowing support in unexpected forms

There was a time when restarting wasn't an option—not externally, anyway.

My mother was eighty-six, widowed, deeply depressed, and in need of assisted living. I moved her 1,300 miles to be closer to me, even though she didn't know a single person nearby.

We did what we could as we waited for an apartment to open. In the meantime, she lived with us.

With her depression, I couldn't leave her alone all day. And it was Christmas—peak season at the gallery. Busy? Absolutely.

So I did what I could think of to do. I took her to work with me. She tried. She couldn't last all day.

That's when the shift happened—not because I had a plan, but because I had to ask.

My cleaning lady stayed and baked cookies with her.

Our gallery handyman took her to the holiday market.

A friend's husband took a day off work and took her bird watching.

It wasn't a system. It wasn't graceful. But it was kindness in action.

Ordinary people stepped in where guilt had been running the show.

Nothing was solved. But something softened. The load didn't disappear. It became shared.

That was the shift.

You can move forward without dropping everything.

You can shift without abandoning anyone.

And you can do it without guilt.

Chapter Four
Tenacity

*Why devotion beats discipline, and how
to stay with what matters when the path
turns uphill, sideways, or sticky*

If resilience is your ability to bounce back, tenacity is your ability to stay.

Not stuck. Not rigid. Not forcing.

Tenacity is the quiet, steady commitment to keep moving in the direction that matters—even when it is humbling, slow, or not turning out quite like you pictured.

Resilience helps you recover when the emotional weather knocks you down.

Tenacity is what keeps you moving once the storm passes—or when it refuses to, learning how to live *within* the storm itself.

Tenacity isn't loud.

It doesn't fist-pump in the mirror at 6 a.m.

It doesn't bark orders or quote sports metaphors.

Tenacity whispers: *Try again. Come closer. Don't give up on yourself yet. Breathe.*

Listen to your internal compass.

Trust when you should stay the course—and when it's time to change direction.

I've met tenacity at every age—sometimes with grace, often with sweat, occasionally with marshmallows, and a side of courage.

Cheerleading Tryouts
#1… and #2… and #3

Tenacity showed up early for me—in a gymnasium that smelled like sneakers and nerves.

When I was a kid, I wanted to be a cheerleader.

Not because I was athletic. Not because I could do a cartwheel without injuring myself.

But because something inside me lit up at the idea of being part of the action.

Junior high? I made it. High school? Entirely different story.

Two suburban junior highs merged into one massive high school—nine hundred ninety-six students in my graduating class alone—part of the urban sprawl of a Detroit subdivision, Redford Township.

I gave the tryout everything I had. Didn't even make the reserve team.

Sophomore year passed. I survived—barely—but cheerleading stayed lodged in my ribcage.

When junior year tryouts loomed, I practiced alone in my backyard, shouting cheers at the cherry tree while birds offered unsolicited commentary from above.

I practiced jumps. Mastered my routine. Built a smile so wide it could've inflated a parade balloon.

And this time? I not only made the squad. I leaped right into varsity.

Not because I suddenly became athletic—but because tenacity sometimes counts more than talent.

It's the steady belief in your own becoming.

Gregg's Green Cabin
AKA: Tenacity Comes in All Forms—Even Woodsmoke

My brother Gregg is only three years older, yet our lifestyles differ by decades.

He splits wood. Turns compost. Hangs laundry on a clothesline year-round—even in blizzards.

He considers this normal. I consider it a frontier documentary.

We live three hours apart, so we usually meet halfway for lunch.

But recently, I drove all the way to his place while he was recovering from knee surgery at seventy.

"So this is your house," I said.

He nodded proudly.

I thought: This is a woodshed with a couch. And yet... he was completely content.

While helping him, I fed the fire, mixed homemade suet outside on a frosty table, and did my best impression of a woman who knew what she was doing.

Somewhere between sorting plastic from paper and the laundry rinsed in recycled gray water, I realized something: It takes tenacity to live a life that truly aligns with you—even if no one else understands it.

Then I noticed a small painting on his end table.

One of mine.

When Mom passed away, he quietly took it from her assisted-living room.

"It's mine now," he'd said, grinning.

I smiled every time I saw it.

Because sometimes tenacity isn't pushing forward.

Sometimes it's holding onto what matters — and letting it remain part of your life.

For Gregg, that painting is belonging.

For me, it's proof that something I created endured.

That it mattered long enough to be carried forward.

Tenacity isn't always effort.

Sometimes it's devotion.

Dale Carnegie, Allison, and the Three C's

Tenacity isn't always physical.

Sometimes it's emotional stewardship—the kind you grow slowly, over years.

When I married Larry, I gained a stepdaughter—but *stepdaughter* never quite fit.

Allison has always been my bonus daughter, especially since we worked side by side in the gallery for twenty-three years.

Working with customers all day meant we needed reinforcements for our attitudes.

Allison and I started reading *How to Win Friends and Influence People* together.

Chapter One: Don't Criticize, Condemn, or Complain.

We read it. Discussed it. Felt spiritually superior.

Moved on to Chapter Two.

Within twenty-four hours, we caught ourselves: complaining about a delivery, criticizing a vendor, condemning a packing slip.

Back to Chapter One.

Chapter Three? Read it. Loved it. Slipped again.

Back to Chapter One.

Chapter Four? You guessed it.

Chapter anything — back to one.

It was maddening. Humbling. And exactly how emotional tenacity works.

Tenacity isn't about getting it right once.

It's about returning to the work, just one more time.

Just like cheerleading. Just like cabins. Just like life.

Lilly's STEM-Class Sparkle

My nine-year-old granddaughter Lilly showed me one of my favorite forms of tenacity—*identity tenacity.*

Picture a STEM classroom—focused on science, technology, engineering, and math—full of practical outfits: ponytails, sweatshirts, sneakers.

Then Lilly walks in wearing:

- a glitter headband
- a white faux-fur vest
- a plastic-beaded necklace
- four rainbow bangles
- and the confidence of a woman entering a gala

She wasn't showing off. She wasn't rebelling. She was simply being herself.

Tenacity, at its core, is staying loyal to who you are—even when the room leans in another direction.

I watched her hold her ground without blinking and thought: *This is what devotion to self looks like.*

No shrinking. No mimicking. No dimming.

She stayed Lilly.

A lesson I didn't learn until much later in life.

The Gallery Marshmallow Experiment

And then—tenacity showed up wearing an apron, knee pads, and a sticky grin.

The marshmallows.

Fourth quarter is a big deal in retail: big events, big inventory, big everything.

One summer, I hired a team member's kids to make hundreds of red paper chains.

They delivered thirty giant leaf bags full.

We created three thirteen-foot, teepee-shaped Christmas trees.

Truly stunning.

But I had nowhere to store them.

We used them once. Still worth it.

The next year, I wanted a fresh idea.

"Let's make it look like it's snowing," I said.

Enter: marshmallow strings.

One marshmallow every six inches, strung on fishing line.

My kitchen counter wasn't long enough, so I ended up crawling commando on the floor like a woman in marshmallow boot camp.

Sticky fingers. Needle pricks. Fishing line unraveling across the house.

At one point, the neighbor's dog burst in, spotted the marshmallows, and chased them like rogue squirrels. Chaos.

But the final display? Magical. The gallery glittered with "snow."

Best year ever.

And we used them again the next year—forming marshmallow teepee trees around the old paper-chain poles.

Sometimes tenacity is simply refusing to give up on an innovative idea just because the first attempt almost became snack-related carnage.

The Real Shape of Tenacity

Tenacity isn't:

- grinding
- forcing
- hustling
- performing
- perfecting
- pushing past capacity into depletion

Tenacity *is*:

- committing with steady devotion
- trying again

- trying differently
- staying curious
- choosing the next right move
- trusting effort even when results aren't visible yet
- being vulnerable

It's not "Show up or else."

It's "Show up because it matters."

Your Tenacity
Already Here

If you've made it this far in life—through heartbreak, illness, recovery, parenting, reinvention, aging, caretaking, and all one hundred forty-seven plot twists adulthood hands you—you are already tenacious.

Not because you pushed harder. But because you stayed:

- through uncertainty
- through weariness
- through questions
- through quiet becoming

Tenacity isn't dramatic. It's directional.

And every time you take a step toward the woman you're becoming, you strengthen it—even when the forecast is uncertain, and your inner compass is clear.

Chapter Five
Confidence

Why confidence isn't a personality trait—it's a practice

If confidence were handed out like party favors, most of us would've grabbed two handfuls, stuffed a few in our purse, and tucked an extra one under our arm for emergencies.

But confidence doesn't work that way.

It's not inherited. It's not gifted. It doesn't arrive in a lightning bolt.

And despite what Facebook promises, it does not magically appear after striking a power pose in your bathroom.

Confidence grows the way a birch tree grows—peeling one layer at a time, quietly, steadily, almost imperceptibly.

Most of my confidence didn't come from succeeding. It came from surviving. From trying. From showing up. From being willing to take the next small, brave step.

Here's the truth: Confidence often begins as a costume—something borrowed from the outside until it grows roots inside you.

My First Lesson in Confidence
The Pediatric Office

The room wasn't just white. It was aggressively white.

White walls. White cupboards. White exam table. White paper. White linoleum.

White, fluorescent light so harsh it buzzed like a mosquito you couldn't swat.

I was a young nurse in my late twenties on my first day at a pediatric office, and that room felt about as welcoming to kids as indoor recess in detention.

But I was "the new girl," so I said nothing.

Weeks passed. Then months.

I settled into the bleached, joyless walls—the way we all acclimate to something that isn't right until it becomes "normal."

Then one morning, a new coworker—older and far braver—walked in, looked around, and said, "These rooms are awful for kids."

With her lead—and the doctor's blessing—we hung whimsical, colorful prints of silly creatures doing silly things.

Instant transformation. A 10% shift.

The rooms moved from sterile to safe. From clinical to cheerful.

And I learned my first lesson in confidence: Confidence often begins with permission—until one day, you realize you're allowed to give it to yourself.

At work, I stayed silent.

At home, I stayed small.

Married to a practical engineer, we bought the sturdy oak table, the sleeper sofa, the sensible appliances I thought were "normal."

Ethan Allen catalogs became fantasy reading, not real life.

I didn't see it then, but what I lacked wasn't money or imagination.

It was confidence.

The confidence to say, *"I want style that feels like me — not what someone else once told me I should want."*

When I Paint, I Wear a Smock

Yes, it keeps me from ruining every shirt I own.

But its real magic is this: When I slip it over my shoulders, I feel braver.

Thirty years ago, my friend Mary—twenty years my senior—gave me my first smock.

Every day in art school, I watched her arthritic hands cradle a paintbrush with tenderness and determination. Mary didn't rush. She didn't apologize. She didn't shrink herself. She painted with a steady, certain kind of grace.

Her tenacity inspired me.

And that smock became a reminder of the strength I saw in her.

So even now, decades later when I button up the front, something inside me straightens.

My breath deepens. My confidence lifts.

It's my confidence cape.

You might be thinking, "All that confidence from a smock?" Oh yes.

Because confidence doesn't always start inside us.

Sometimes we borrow it—from a ritual, a color, a garment, a memory—until it grows roots within us. And there is no shame in that.

Sometimes the bravest thing we can do is let something outside us remind us who we are inside.

So I'll ask you: What's your confidence trigger?

Your red heels?

Your briefcase?

That lipstick you only wear when you mean business?

Whatever it is, be like my grandmother.

Her confidence trigger was her suitcase-sized purse she carried everywhere.

And if necessary, she was known to use it as a battering ram.

It was her badge of honor.

So whatever it is for you: Wear it. Use it. Let it lift you.

Your confidence deserves every tool it can get.

Confidence Looks Like Ease
Aislynn and the Art of Knowing What to Press

I could never keep up with the pace of social media—or technology in general—if it weren't for a lesson my granddaughter, Aislynn, taught me.

Instagram had just released Reels, and once again, I felt a hundred steps behind, staring at my phone with no idea which button to press.

One afternoon, all three grandkids were at my house, not especially excited about doing something thoughtful for their dad for Father's Day. But sometimes all it takes is a nudge.

I handed each of them several blank sheets of printer paper and a marker, assigned a single word, and instructed them to write one letter per page. Then we headed to the park.

There, I handed my phone to eleven-year-old Aislynn and asked, "Can you use this app and make a video of the boys, each holding up a letter?"

"Sure," she said—despite not having a phone of her own and never having used the app.

Liam wedged himself between two tree branches holding up the **A**—yes, the *A*, even though it was supposed to be the **H** in *Happy Father's Day*. No one noticed. We kept going.

Jude slid down the slide.

Liam rocked on the bouncing horse.

Then swung from the monkey bars.

Spun on the merry-go-round.

Each time holding up a letter.

When my phone battery died halfway through, Aislynn didn't blink.

"We'll finish at your house."

What? I live in a condo with a minimal backyard. No park props.

Aislynn proved me wrong.

A roll down a hill.

Popping out of a bush.

Even staging a reveal—burying the letter under bark, then filming as they swished it aside.

When Aislynn declared the project done, I watched in awe.

She tapped, trimmed, edited, added music—including getting the letters in order—and somehow made fireworks explode at the end.

Calm. Steady. No second-guessing.

The lesson wasn't about technology.

It was about confidence.

About trusting yourself enough to move forward—without needing to know everything first.

So now, when it comes to tech?

I know exactly who to ask.

Jude's "I FEEL HANDSOME!" Lesson

When my grandson Jude was three, he decided to dress himself.

The outfits were... imaginative.

He'd waddle in wearing his older brother's too-big shirt, inside-out pants, mismatched socks, and a grin so wide it could've powered a small city.

Every morning he'd ask, "Do I look handsome?"

And every morning I answered, "If you feel handsome, you look handsome."

By day three, he didn't even ask. He strutted in, chest puffed out, and declared, "I FEEL HANDSOME!"

Confidence, at its heart, isn't about how things appear.

It's about how you feel inside your own skin.

As adults, we forget this. We become tangled in comparison charts, productivity meters, social media, and other people's opinions.

The more important question is: How do I feel?

Am I standing in my truth—or in someone else's approval?

Jude understood something instinctively it took me decades to learn: **Confidence is a feeling before it is a skill.**

And a lesson that arrives when the student is ready.

Confidence Is Evidence, Not Magic

People assume confident women are born that way. Not me.

Confidence doesn't come from personality.

It comes from practice—over a lifetime.

From cheerleading. To nursing. To continuing to paint—even when nothing sold at my first solo show.

From tiny pieces of evidence that slowly build a larger truth:

I can do this.

I survived that.

I didn't crumble.

I didn't run.

I came back.

Confidence grows from:

- sending the email you're afraid to send
- speaking up when your voice trembles
- painting the first stroke
- painting the last stroke
- launching the idea, invention, or policy you might be judged for
- setting one strong boundary
- asking for help
- telling the truth
- stepping back into your life after losing your footing

Confidence is a side effect of living—not flawlessly, but fully.

The Inside-Out / Outside-In Loop

Confidence is built from both directions.

Inside-out:
- self-trust
- self-compassion
- self-respect
- honoring your needs

Outside-in:
- evidence
- practice
- experience
- validation through a compliment that sneaks into your heart

We need both.

Outside-in gives you courage. Inside-out gives you encouragement.

Together?

Confidence becomes sustainable instead of situational.

Your Confidence
Already Growing

If you're reading this book, something inside you is already opening.

You're noticing things. Listening to whispers. Craving something truer.

That's confidence beginning.

Confidence doesn't start after you've "arrived."

It starts here—

in the wanting.

In the curiosity.

In the trying.

In the decision to stop apologizing for taking up space in your own life.

Here's the truth I want you to hold close:

You do not become confident and then begin.

You begin—and that is what builds confidence.

Your confidence is a living, breathing thing.

And it grows every time you take even the smallest step toward who you really are.

Over and over again.

Chapter Six
Bravery Comes in Sizes

Why bravery isn't loud or showy —
it simply moves you forward

For most of my life, I thought bravery belonged to bold people:

- skydivers
- rock climbing
- emergency responders

Meanwhile, my bravery looked more like:

- calling the dentist back
- wearing a swimsuit before June
- asking the salesperson for a different size
- admitting I needed help

We assume courage should feel dramatic — or at least look impressive from the outside. If our heart isn't pounding or someone isn't watching, we dismiss it as ordinary.

For a long time, I didn't recognize my own small acts of bravery either.

One of them showed up during Tulip Time.

If you've ever been to Holland, Michigan, during the festival, you know the streets are packed, the sidewalks crowded, and parking spots guarded like treasure. I found myself downtown, inching along in traffic, when I spotted an opening just large enough to tempt me.

Parallel parking has never been my strength. Add festival crowds, a line of cars waiting behind me, and the unspoken pressure of "don't mess this up," and I felt that familiar urge to keep driving.

But I didn't.

I took a breath. Put the car in reverse. And parked.

It wasn't graceful. No one clapped. I didn't emerge victorious. But I had chosen to stay instead of escape, to try instead of circle the block indefinitely.

At the time, it felt less like bravery and more like survival. But looking back, I can see it for what it was: a small decision to move forward instead of away.

That's when I began to understand that bravery isn't about bravado.

It's about direction.

Bravery is often quiet. Unremarkable. Measured in inches, not leaps.

It's the decision to stay in the conversation.

To ask the question.

To take the next step — even when your confidence hasn't caught up yet.

What I know now is this: Bravery comes in sizes.

All valid. All worthy.

Tiny brave. Medium brave. Big brave.

And the sneaky brave that doesn't look brave at all until years later.

Bravery in Adulthood
Adam & Brian

I have two sons.

Brian — the oldest — is married, juggles a civil engineering job, and lives in a Michigan subdivision with three young kids bouncing around.

Adam — my youngest — hangs his hat in Lake Tahoe. He's lived off the grid, harvested rainwater, and once trained llamas — yes, the tall, toothy kind that spit when they disagree.

He's done roughly one million things that would terrify me.

And yet, Adam shakes his head at Brian's kid chaos and says, "When the washing machine eats a $100 ballet leotard, floods the basement, and Brian stays patient? That's brave."

He's right.

Bravery is personal.

And it doesn't need to look the same to be real — even within the same family.

Sometimes bravery isn't climbing mountains.

Sometimes it's folding laundry when you'd rather be golfing.

Sometimes bravery looks like:

- staying when you want to bolt—or leaving when you want to stay
- trying again after the first attempt flops
- responding gently when your nerves want to snap
- saying, "I'll handle it," even when you'd rather hide in your car

This is adult bravery.

Quiet. Steady. Directional.

Karol's Pond vs. Lake Michigan

Growing up in Detroit, water meant swimming pools—concrete, chlorine, and the smell of sunscreen.

Years later, living steps from Lake Michigan, I fell in love with vastness—the kind of beauty that hushes your whole body.

Then I met my friend Karol. She raved—*raved*—about the pond behind her house. The pond.

Not the lake. Not the horizon. Not the dramatic waves that could knock a grown man sideways.

A pond.

I smiled politely, but inside I thought, *How can a pond compete with Lake Michigan?*

Then I downsized.

My new condo sat beside—you guessed it—a pond.

On my first morning, fog kissed the surface. Light rippled across the water like a secret. Clouds drifted in reflection.

And I felt it.

Calm. Quiet. A restart.

Karol had been right all along. It isn't the size of the water that matters. It's the stillness it brings.

Bravery works the same way.

You don't have to swim Lake Michigan to be brave.

Some days bravery is sitting beside a pond, letting your shoulders ease, and resetting yourself.

And on other days, a Lake Michigan horizon helps you remember how to inhale fully again.

Both count.

Both are brave.

Effort Over Certainty

Most recently, I'd been trying to think creatively outside the box. But I was stuck inside one.

Or should I say—inside a rectangle?

The Tulip Time Festival poster deadline was fast approaching.

The format was strict: 16 x 20 inches. No bigger. No smaller.

After painting tulips for thirty years, every brushstroke started to look the same.

Safe. Predictable.

And the clock was ticking—one week until submissions were due.

Then I stumbled into something unexpected: a self-defense class.

My inner critic wasted no time. Too old. Too clumsy. Crazy.

But I went anyway. Because, maybe, just maybe, I could discover something I could teach my granddaughter.

That awkward class ended up teaching me more about painting than I expected.

It wasn't about perfect form. It was about effort. About trying when you'd rather play it safe.

Being brave enough to learn a few safety moves turned into curiosity in a paint smock.

What if I tried something new?

What if I fell flat—but what if I discovered a spark?

That week, I traded safe brushstrokes for fresh ideas.

If I don't get accepted, at least I wouldn't be left wondering: *What if I had tried?*

After fifteen years of painting with oils and a palette knife, I set them aside.

I picked up brushes. Acrylics. Black ink lines that curved and moved in ways my work never had before.

I didn't win.

But I made the top twenty.

At any age, in any season, the question that moves us forward is the same: *What if...?*

The Camping Boys
Bravery by Duct Tape

When my sons were young, our summer vacations were camping.

We borrowed my dad's travel trailer—roughly the size of a toaster with wheels.

The kitchenette unfolded into a bed.

The bathroom required entering backwards if you wanted any hope of sitting.

But the boys loved it.

And honestly? For this city girl, the sound of rain pinging on a tin roof beats a soggy tent every day of the week.

One summer, the boys discovered a pile of leftover wood in an abandoned lot:

- two long two-by-fours
- several short, uneven pieces
- and one bewildered mother thinking, What on earth are they planning to build?

They sprinted back to the trailer and grabbed my "toolbox," which consisted of:

- a hammer
- a screwdriver
- a handful of mismatched nails

• and my sacred roll of duct tape. (The single-mother survival kit—though let's be clear, I was the only one who ever used duct tape.)

The boys preferred ambition, enthusiasm, and the creative misuse of nails.

Plan A: The Oak-Tree Ladder

They hammered together a ladder and leaned it against a tall oak to spy on other campers. It was great. Until it wasn't.

A fearless five-year-old from the next site shimmied up the tree like a caffeinated squirrel.

Plan A: shattered.

Plan B: The Frog Dock

They declared the crooked structure a "dock" and dragged it to a pond, butterfly nets in hand.

The frogs remained unimpressed quickly heading for deeper water.

Plan B: abandoned.

Plan C: Mini Golf in the Sand

Their masterpiece.

Using every scrap of wood, they built a sandy mini-golf course complete with:

- wobbly bridges
- lopsided tunnels
- and a swinging trap rigged with dental floss (Because we couldn't find string—and apparently cavities are less frightening than supply shortages.)

They swung that hammer like they were building Rome.

Watching them—sandy, sweaty, determined—I realized something: Bravery isn't about perfection. It's about devotion.

It's trying something new with whatever tools you have—even if those tools are mismatched nails and a questionable plan.

That summer, my boys taught me something important: I didn't need to have everything figured out. I just needed to be willing.

What Bravery Really Is

Bravery isn't:

- loud
- flashy
- reckless
- dramatic
- something other people have

Bravery is:

- choosing kindness over convenience
- speaking truth softly
- retrying after embarrassment

- walking into a room where no one knows your name
- allowing a new version of yourself to emerge
- trusting that your way of seeing things matters—even when it's different
- beginning again

Bravery isn't a roar. It's a direction.

Your Bravery
Already Here

If you're reading this book, you're brave.

You're choosing self-awareness over self-abandonment.

You're listening to whispers you once brushed aside.

You're wanting something truer, deeper, gentler.

That wanting? That's bravery.

Bravery doesn't begin after you've succeeded.

It begins the moment you ask:

- What now?
- What's next?
- What do I need?

Every small brave action you choose points you toward the woman you're becoming.

And trust me—she is worth following.

PART III
STRENGTHENING YOUR RESILIENCE

Chapter Seven
What You Believe and Why It Matters

Why losing yourself isn't failure—it's a sign you're ready to be found

If you had met me in my late teens or early twenties and asked, "Who are you?"

I would've answered with confidence.

Not about who I was—but about who I hoped to become.

(Which, in hindsight, should've been my first clue.)

I would've said things like:

- "I'm going to get married."
- "I'll be a homemaker like my mom."
- "I'll raise kids."
- "I'll have a happy, suburban life."

Not because those dreams were wrong.

But because they were inherited—wrapped in ribbons of expectation, tradition, and my mother's steady voice saying, "Kathleen, it's a beautiful life."

And it *is* a good life.

It just wasn't fully mine. Not yet.

What I didn't understand then was this: Feeling overwhelmed isn't a personal flaw.

It's information. It's data. It's measurable. It's part of our internal GPS system.

It's a quiet signal that your life is rubbing against the edges of a self you haven't fully met.

And my edges? Oh, they were sharp.

The "Should" That Shaped My Life

I became a nurse for the most romantic reason a young woman can have: A high school sweetheart who didn't propose.

He was headed to Michigan Tech to study forestry—ecosystems, sustainability, and a future he could name.

I was headed toward... nothing solid.

So when my mom said, "Kathleen, nursing is perfect. You'll always have a job. You can work *anywhere*."

I heard a different promise entirely.

Anywhere meant I could follow him.

Anywhere meant I could build my life around him.

Anywhere meant I could still reach the dream I'd been groomed to want:

Marriage -> home -> kids -> happiness.

It was a very tidy equation. Life, unfortunately, is not.

I admired my homemaker mother.

Her joy. Her devotion. Her pride.

I assumed:

- I should want the same things.
- I should feel fulfilled by the same path.
- I should find happiness the way she did.

I didn't yet realize that *should* is often the first symptom of identity confusion.

The Life That Looked Perfect—But Didn't Fit

Years later, I checked every box:

- ☐ marriage
- ☐ toddlers

□   a two-story house with a neat little picket fence
□   a one-day-a-week nursing job that looked ideal from the outside
□   a life that appeared exactly as it should

And inside? I was quietly unraveling.

I'd stand in that substantial house and ask myself, "What exactly is wrong with me?"

Not out loud—I didn't have that kind of courage yet—but in the private, echoing chambers of my mind.

How could I feel restless, confused, or unhappy when everything looked so perfect on paper? Guilt and shame braided together like a rope.

What I didn't yet understand was this: Nothing was wrong.

I simply wasn't living the life that belonged to me.

I was living the life I inherited.

Reaching for the Wrong Rescue

When you don't know who you are, you often reach outward.

You search for something—anything—that might fill the hollow inside.

For me, that reaching came as attention that felt like validation, affection that felt like oxygen, and a promise ring that felt like certainty.

I believed in this fresh-start promise of being together so fully that I followed him 1,000 miles.

Yes, the move from Michigan to North Dakota that I mentioned earlier.

It was the same misdirected longing of a young woman trying to outrun her own emptiness—though I didn't know it at the time.

For sixty-three days, I believed someone else would hand me happiness.

Sixty-three days from arrival to goodbye.

Then he told me to leave. Just like that.

No roses. No promises. No happily ever after.

Shame became my new partner.

My identity too fragile to move back home.

I moved into a basement apartment.

Overwhelm and humiliation became my new roommates.

What followed was a painful unraveling that cost me a marriage and reshaped my understanding of love—a story I tell more fully elsewhere. But what matters here is what came after.

A landlord named Marge—the woman you met earlier—who whisked me off to the college art department and somehow offered more emotional stability than I'd ever known.

It was rock bottom.

And the solid foundation of everything that came next.

The Basement Apartment and the Beginning of Me

When you've never done it before, there's something strange about being completely alone.

No expectations. No roles to perform. No versions of yourself to maintain.

Just you. Raw. Bruised. Honest.

In that basement apartment—cement walls, meatloaf drifting through the vents—I realized something essential: You cannot outsource your identity.

Not to a partner. Not to a job. Not to a fantasy.

You have to belong to yourself first. And I didn't. Not yet.

But this is where I began learning how.

A First Practice: Noticing What Lights You Up

When I returned to college, I didn't march onto campus with confidence.

I tiptoed—like someone returning borrowed courage.

I majored in business because it felt safe.

Predictable. Responsible.

And then I took a required elective: Basic Drawing 101.

That class didn't just open a door—it swung it off its hinges.

The pencils. The smudges. The quiet focus.

The way shapes slowly became something real.

It felt like coming home to a part of myself I didn't know I'd misplaced.

Here was the first micro-practice I didn't know I was putting into play: Notice what gives you energy instead of draining it.

Not what impresses others. Not what looks good on paper.

Just this simple question: *What feels like I can breathe?*

That question became a breadcrumb trail back to myself.

A 10% shift.

Overwhelm Isn't a Breakdown—It's a Breakthrough

Here's what I know now: Overwhelm doesn't mean you're failing.

It means you're outgrowing something.

It's the signal that the life you're living no longer matches the woman you're becoming.

You feel lost because you're leaving an old identity.

You feel ashamed because you think you should know better.

You feel stuck because you're carrying beliefs that were never yours.

That confusion? It's the doorway.

And clarity? Clarity is what waits on the other side.

Your Beliefs
A Gentle Inventory

Here's a simple noticing ritual—no journaling required unless it's your thing.

When something feels heavy, ask yourself:

- Is this mine—or was it handed to me?
- Does this belief bring relief—or pressure?
- Does this path feel aligned—or merely expected?

You're not looking for answers all at once. You're simply learning to notice that there are questions.

This is how resilience strengthens—not through force, but through awareness.

Your Overwhelm
Reframed

If you're reading this and recognizing yourself:

- the shame of "having everything"
- the guilt of wanting something different
- the fear of seeming ungrateful
- the ache of not recognizing yourself anymore

Hear this clearly.

You are not broken.

You are not dramatic.

You are not ungrateful.

You are not failing.

You are shedding.

You are shifting.

You are waking up to yourself.

The old structure of your life can no longer contain the size of your becoming.

That's not a crisis. That's information.

And when you learn to read it — gently, honestly, without judgment — it becomes direction.

This is how belief changes. Not all at once. But enough to move you forward.

One thought questioned.

One truth reclaimed.

One 10% shift at a time.

Chapter Eight
Give Up Perfection

Why "good enough" is a gift, and imperfection is how real life breathes

If perfection had a mascot, she'd be named **Exhausted**.

She'd be the woman smoothing couch pillows before sitting down, rewriting the grocery list because her handwriting slanted, and triple-checking a text message because emojis suddenly feel like a legal contract.

For a long stretch of my life, I was that woman.

I thought being "perfect" made me prepared. Responsible. Worthy.

But here's the truth I wish someone had whispered to me sooner: Perfection isn't preparation. It's pressure. And it's one of the fastest ways to feel inadequate in a life you're actually living beautifully.

Giving up perfectionism isn't about lowering your standards.

It's about choosing where your energy goes — like spending emotional currency.

Here's how I learned — and relearned — this, one imperfect moment at a time.

Liam's Birthday Fiasco
AKA: The Pinterest-Perfect Plan That Tried to Kill Me

It was my grandson Liam's thirteenth birthday, and I had one job: Lunch.

Simple. Or so I thought.

I prepped ahead. Menu. Decorations. Gift.

Even layered Jell-O into crystal brandy glasses, ribbons of color glistening like stained glass. My grandson is a devoted Jell-O lover, and I could already picture his smile when he spotted them on the table.

I packed the coolers and drove to my son's house — lunch carefully timed between a soccer game and a clay-pigeon outing.

And then:

I forgot the ice cream at home.

I grabbed curry chicken instead of the pizza-burger filling.

I used leftover taco meat instead, added oregano, and called it "gourmet."

I sprinted to the store for ice cream.

Returned to an escaped parrot squawking like a security alarm.

Took a series of blurry photos because nothing — and no one — held still.

And the grand finale?

I forgot to serve the rainbow Jell-O entirely. Not one crystal-glass masterpiece made it out of the cooler. And yet?

We had a ball. Laughter. Chaos.

Stories we still retell.

And we made it to the shooting range on time.

That day taught me something essential about resilience: When perfection falls apart, presence steps in — *if you make room for it.*

If you've ever had a day like my birthday-lunch fiasco, try this micro-choice: Instead of asking, *"How did I mess this up?"* Ask, *"What actually matters right now?"*

That's energy management.

That's boundary-setting with reality.

That's resilience in real life.

Jude's Scribble Lesson

One afternoon, I had my five-year-old grandson Jude buckled into his booster seat for a thirty-minute drive.

He wanted my phone. I wanted him to use his imagination.

I had forgotten the travel bag of activities, so I handed him a plain notebook and a basic ballpoint pen from the console.

He sighed. This was not exciting.

But by the time we reached my house, he'd filled page after page with scribbles.

Circles. Mazes. Dots. Swirls.

Nothing planned. Nothing polished. Nothing perfect.

He didn't say.

"I'm not good at drawing."

"I don't know how."

"This isn't turning out right."

He just started.

And right then, I thought: I want to be like Jude.

To begin without negotiating with perfection first.

To let the process lead.

To trust movement more than outcome.

That's a daily practice of self-trust. When perfection tells you to wait, resilience whispers: *start anyway.*

My Rust-and-Green Volkswagen
AKA: Strong Enough

My first car after nursing school was a used Volkswagen — rust and green, but mostly rust.

Not cute. Not impressive. Not even warm.

Rain leaked through the floorboard, so I bought a heavy-duty suction-cup mat to avoid sitting in a puddle.

In Minnesota winters, the heater was so unreliable the car turned into an igloo.

My solution?

I plugged in a space heater on a timer so it would thaw before my 7 a.m. shift.

Was it perfect? Not even close.

But it started. It got me to work. It carried me through a season when my confidence was fragile and my wallet thinner than a dime.

And here's the truth that matters:

Dependable beats perfect. Because dependable lets you move.

Perfect keeps you frozen.

This is where boundaries come in.

Sometimes resilience means saying: "This is good enough — for now. And knowing it's not forever." That decision saves your energy for what actually matters.

The Real Definition of Letting Go

Perfectionism convinces you that if you could just do everything right, life would stop hurting.

But perfection never prevents pain. It only prevents progress.

Let go of perfection when:

- the room is a little messy
- the plan needs rescuing
- the photo is blurry
- the gift is late
- the cake is lopsided
- the outfit is wrinkled
- the day goes sideways
- and Jell-O stays in the cooler

Perfectionism isn't protection.

It's paralysis.

Letting go isn't giving up.

It's choosing where to place your care.

That choice — again and again — is how resilience strengthens.

A Simple Daily Practice: Choose "Enough"

Here's a livable ritual you can try — journaling optional.

Once a day, notice where perfection is draining you.

Then ask:

- What would "enough" look like here?
- What am I protecting by trying to be perfect?
- What could I release without harm?

And then — this part matters — Act on that answer.

Send the email.

Leave the dish.

Rest your body.

Say no kindly.

Say yes imperfectly.

That's not laziness. That's wisdom.

Your Imperfect Resilience
Already Here

If you're reading this, you've already lived through imperfect moments.

You've:

- adjusted
- improvised
- fixed what you could
- laughed when it wasn't funny
- recovered from plans that fell apart
- loved people in the middle of chaos
- and kept going

That's not failure. That's humanity.

Perfection is a myth. Presence is a miracle.

Your life doesn't need to be flawless to be beautiful.

It just needs to be lived.

So today—Let it be enough. Let it be imperfect. Let it be real.

Give up perfection. And feel how much lighter resilience becomes when you do.

Chapter Nine
Humor Heals

Why laughter loosens the grip of hard things

If emotional growth had a secret weapon, it wouldn't be discipline.

Or willpower.

Or inspirational quotes painted on reclaimed barn wood.

It would be laughter. Real laughter.

The kind that surprises you.

The kind that unplugs your shoulders from your ears.

The kind that loosens something in your chest you didn't even realize was tight.

Humor isn't frivolous. It isn't immature. And it isn't avoidance.

Humor is a release valve. A softening agent.

A tiny door out of overwhelm.

And if your life looks anything like mine, you've needed that tiny door more than once.

The Drywall Hopper Disaster
When Laughter Is the Only Choice Left

When we first opened the gallery, we watched every nickel. Building the display walls? Larry decided he could handle that himself.

For the project, he needed a contraption called a drywall hopper—imagine a paint gun with a giant funnel on top, filled with wet paste and Styrofoam pellets that looked exactly like popcorn.

He handed me a giant piece of cardboard. "Kate, stand here. Hold this. I don't know how far this stuff shoots."

I stood there, dutifully holding my cardboard shield, channeling the courage of a woman about to be the target at an axe-throwing contest.

Larry pulled the trigger. The hopper roared. The air shook. I jumped.

And the spray? It didn't hit the wall. It didn't hit the cardboard.

It hit me. Head to toe. Cold, wet, smelly drywall paste dripping off my chin.

There is a moment in every woman's life when she must choose between screaming—and laughing.

I chose laughing. Not because it was funny.

But because laughing was the only way for it to *become* funny.

That day taught me something I've carried ever since: Humor gives you a way out when everything else feels like a mess.

The Flypaper Haircut

One September, black flies invaded our basement frame shop—biting, buzzing, plotting our demise. Larry, bless him, hung a strip of flypaper in the bathroom, hoping for relief.

Later, I heard a crash—followed by language that would curl a bishop's hair. The bathroom door flew open. Out stormed Larry... with flypaper stuck to his head.

It was not the haircut he wanted. But it was definitely the one he got.

And oh, did I laugh. On the inside. Safely and silently. Which, sometimes, feels just as good.

Because every now and then, humor is the only thing that can rescue a Tuesday.

The Gift That Rattled
When Laughter Loosens Something

While owning the gallery, I had a repeat customer named Michael who purchased three of four elegant glass pieces displayed as a set.

Disappointed that the collection would be split, I asked if he'd like the fourth piece at a special price.

He declined. "Three are perfect," he said. "They're a Christmas gift for my wife, Mary."

I wrapped the pieces individually in our signature birch paper and ribbon.

A short while later, Michael called back. He'd decided to take the fourth piece after all.

I had a brilliant idea. Surely Mary deserved one present that wasn't identical to the others.

So I grabbed a palm-sized box, filled it with broken scraps of picture-frame glass, sealed it shut, and tucked it inside the outer gift box with the delicate bowl. Then I wrapped the whole thing in festive paper from my personal stash.

When Mary picked it up, her gift would rattle.

A surprise. A joke. A moment of delight.

Shortly, Michael returned and I enthusiastically handed him the wrapped box, proudly explaining how surprised Mary would be on Christmas morning.

He paused. "The gift," he said carefully, "is for my secretary."

The joke was on me.

Then he smiled. "But it's perfect. Barbara has a wonderful sense of humor. She'll love it."

And I did something rare—and freeing. I laughed. Fully.

Not defensively. Not politely.

But with a belly laugh that acknowledged my assumption, my misstep, and my very human moment.

That laugh stayed with me.

Because learning to laugh at yourself isn't humiliation—it's humility.

And humility keeps the heart soft.

Shared Laughter Pulls Hearts Closer Together

"You did what?" I asked my eighty-two-year-old neighbor, Bob.

"Skydiving."

"From a plane?"

"Yup. If I waited until I felt confident to live my life, I'd never have lived. So I pretended I wasn't scared. This time, I told myself I was Tom Cruise. It worked."

I thought of Bob later when my son Adam—my extreme-sports guy who snowboards off-grid in Lake Tahoe—asked me to paint a bear for his cabin.

I'd painted for him before. Landscapes. Water. Mountains.

No animals. No people.

Still, Bob's words rang in my ears. *If I waited until I felt confident, I'd never live.*

So I dove in. I painted a bear—mostly the head—big, bold colors, heavy texture.

Adam gave it the once-over. "It looks like a fox."

I roared with laughter. What else could I do?

That laugh mattered.

Laughter spared us defensiveness.

Laughter kept the moment light.

Laughter protected our connection.

I started again. This time, a vertical piece: one sturdy aspen among towering pines. Perched in the tree—a tiny baby bear. On the ground—mama bear, much smaller than the head portrait, but unmistakable.

This one passed inspection.

More importantly, it felt good that I'd lived. That I'd tried. Missed. Laughed.

And stayed open anyway.

Laughter Is a Soft Place to Land

Humor isn't avoidance. It's resilience wearing a smile.

Laughter:

- settles the nervous system
- loosens emotional grip
- reroutes the brain away from pressure, perfection, and panic
- releases feel-good chemistry—endorphins, serotonin, dopamine

Laughing at:

- the mess
- the mishap
- the misunderstanding
- the moment gone sideways

Laughing...lets joy back in.

It widens your emotional doorway.

And most of us have been living with doors shut far too tightly.

A Gentle Practice: Let Humor Interrupt

Here's a small, livable practice—no performance required.

When you feel yourself tightening, ask:

- Is there a lighter way to hold this?
- What part of this might be funny later?
- What happens if I don't take this quite so personally?

You're not dismissing the moment.

You're giving yourself room to breathe.

Humor doesn't erase hard things. It helps you survive them without hardening.

Sometimes laughter arrives immediately. Sometimes it comes later. Both count.

Your Lightness
Already Inside You

If you're here—reading this chapter—you've already had moments when laughter saved you.

When humor softened a hard day.

When absurdity loosened your worry.

When something imperfect became unforgettable.

Levity is not childish. It's wise. It's mature. It's what keeps your heart open when life gives you reasons to close it.

And it's always there, waiting to be noticed—even in drywall paste, even in flypaper, even when the joke turns gently back on you.

Your laughter is a lifeline. And you deserve to grab it.

Chapter Ten
Growth Needs Motion and Patience

Why waiting is not passive—it's powerful

If resilience is bending and tenacity is staying, then patience is breathing.

Not the calm, Zen-master breathing, meditation apps talk about.

I mean the real kind — the kind where you grit your teeth a little, try not to scream, breathe, and whisper to yourself, *just... hold... on.*

Because here's the truth no one tells you:

Patience isn't stillness.

It's strength.

It's staying present long enough for something good, or true, or necessary to unfold.

I learned this slowly — in my teens, in my parenting, in my gallery, in my paint — and in places I didn't expect, like a public park and a 5K race I had absolutely no business running.

And I should tell you this up front:

Patience is the trait I have to practice most.

Not because I don't believe in it — but because it does not come naturally to me.

We live in a world that rewards speed.

Faster internet.

Faster health diagnoses through virtual calls.

Faster home delivery — sometimes before I've even finished my coffee.

And I am, by nature, a *why-isn't-this-done-yet* kind of person.

I felt this most acutely when I owned the gallery. We tracked sales daily, hoping to outpace the year before. But art doesn't behave like gift-shop inventory. Some days we sold a large original painting. Other days, nothing but a handful of ten-dollar journals.

On those slower days, patience meant coaching myself not to panic — not to compare — and to trust the longer arc of the month instead of the mood of the day. A single quiet Tuesday didn't mean failure; the month's rhythm told the real story.

Even now, I have to remind myself: growth doesn't respond to urgency.

I still catch myself wanting instant results.

Why can't five pounds disappear in a week?

I only had one apple fritter.

(I tend to forget the part about exercise.)

Patience, for me, is not passive.

It's learned.

Practiced.

And often disguised as play, color, and waiting longer than feels comfortable.

These stories are how I learned that.

Hide-and-Seek at the Playground
Patience Disguised as Play

It was a golden summer day, the kind where the air feels like an exhale.

My two grandsons and I parked our bikes at a crowded rack and headed for the playground.

The place hummed—dogs barking, kids squealing, sunlight catching the monkey bars just right.

After an hour, the inevitable call came.

"Can we go home?"

But I knew what *home* meant. Screens.

"Let's play hide-and-seek," I said.

Off they darted—behind slides, trees, tunnels—burning off scraps of energy.

By the fourth round, Jude—seven years old and imaginative as a kid building castles out of couch cushions—had run out of hiding places. Panic flickered across his face.

I scanned the cluttered bike rack. "Stand right in the middle," I whispered. "You'll blend in. You're wearing the same colors as all the bikes and gear. Just stay still."

He blinked. Then stepped into the rack and froze like a statue.

His older brother, Liam, counted loudly. "READY OR NOT, HERE I COME!"

Then he searched everywhere. Trees. Swings. Under the slide. He walked past Jude three times.

I held my breath harder than Jude did. But Jude stayed still. Absolutely still.

A tiny lesson in patience stood right there among the Schwinns and Huffys.

That single moment stretched our park time by twenty minutes—and the retelling of the "epic hide" bought us many more.

Patience doesn't always look like discipline.

Sometimes it looks like a seven-year-old standing perfectly still in a bike rack while the whole world buzzes around him.

Jude didn't win by being faster or louder — he won by staying, trusting, and waiting long enough for success to find him.

And sometimes, that's exactly what success looks like.

The Color Run
Patience Disguised as Courage

The word *run* has never belonged anywhere near my name.

Walking? Yes. Jogging up gallery stairs? Sure. Running a race? Ha.

Then my bonus daughter, Allison, printed out a Couch-to-5K schedule, circled a date, and said, "It's just a 5K. Lilly already said she'd run it. Want to join us?"

My seven-year-old granddaughter was doing the run. With or without me. Against all logic, I said yes.

Even the training plan carried a red flag — the word *run*.

Walk for ninety seconds. Run for a minute. Walk for two minutes. Run for a minute.

On paper, it looked like a staircase with no railing — 4,500 steps high.

Every cell in my body protested — until something surprising happened.

I stopped looking at the staircase and focused only on the step in front of me. One walk-jog at a time. One day at a time. One *please let me survive this* prayer at a time.

Race day arrived. And I kept pace with my granddaughter—both of us laughing, sweating, cheering each other on.

Then came the color cannons—pink, blue, yellow exploding around us. I looked like an exploded bag of Skittles. And it was glorious.

Patience isn't slow. It's steady.

It's letting progress happen in small, doable increments—until one day you look up and realize you're running beside your granddaughter in a cloud of rainbow powder and loving every minute of it.

The Tulip Time Challenge
Patience Disguised as Persistence

Prints, stripes, lace, checks—fabric scraps gathered from seamstresses who sewed the authentic Dutch costumes for my city's third-largest flower festival.

Perfect, I thought, for a collage painting to submit to the Tulip Time poster contest.

I layered paint. Glued fabric. Rearranged. Re-glued. Rearranged again.

Some fabric dissolved. Some turned transparent. Some curled like they were trying to escape. My fingertips stayed tacky. My studio table looked like a fabric tornado had touched down.

Every time frustration peaked, the colors whispered me back. So I stayed. And stayed.

Weeks later, I scraped everything off the table. Underneath the chaos was one draft— a single tulip waiting to be born.

I abandoned the fabric scraps. Poured paint. Dabbed brushes. Even a risky finger smudge here and there. Relief moved through my hands.

I submitted it. I won the 2022 honor.

Not because everything went smoothly—but because I waited long enough to find the painting inside the mess.

That's patience. Not passive waiting— active trusting.

The Real Shape of Patience

Patience isn't:

- forcing calm

- pretending you're fine
- waiting silently while boiling inside

Patience is:

- letting time soften what pressure can't
- doing the next gentle thing
- trusting the process
- giving your nervous system a minute
- believing that stuck isn't forever

Patience doesn't rush. It simply says: *Stay. Something good is forming.*

Your Patience
Already Here

If you've ever stayed, waited, softened, paused, or breathed through uncertainty—you already know patience.

You don't become patient by willing yourself into serenity.

You become patient by living—and choosing, again and again, not to run from the process shaping you.

And here's the truth I want you to carry forward: Nothing is late.

Not your clarity. Not your support. Not what's coming next.

A 10% shift— at just the right moment.

PART IV
LET LIFE EXPAND YOU

Chapter Eleven
Find Your Supports

Why no restart thrives in isolation — and why the people who show up (and the ones who don't) shape your courage

If resilience helps you bounce back, and tenacity keeps you moving forward, then support is what holds you steady in the middle—the invisible scaffolding that keeps you upright when life wobbles.

Support isn't always loud. It isn't always obvious.

And it doesn't always come from who you expect.

But when it's there? You feel it all the way to your bones.

I used to think being strong meant doing everything myself.

Then life kindly—and repeatedly—proved me wrong.

Here are a few of the ways support has shown up for me—in moments that were messy, magical, soggy, and sky-blue.

Soaked in the Moment
When Support Arrives on Four Paws
and Drags You Into the Rain.

Sadie—the neighbor's black Lab—woke me at midnight with a wet nose and a whine.

I gave in: mismatched pajamas, bedhead, bare feet.

Out we went into the quiet cul-de-sac so she could do her business.

Then she tugged me toward the golf course, tail high, absolutely certain we were taking a walk at 12:07 a.m.—while I wondered why I had said yes to dog sitting.

Halfway down the street, the sky broke open. Not a drizzle. Not a sprinkle. A biblical downpour.

There I stood, drenched, glowing like a neon sign under the streetlight, staring at a dog who was delighted by the chaos—snapping at raindrops like they were snacks.

A few years ago, I would've been frustrated. At the rain. At myself. At the whole ridiculous moment.

But midlife teaches you something tender: Regret is heavier than rain.

So I laughed. And kept laughing. Sadie spun in circles, tail a blur.

And I realized—in the middle of that midnight monsoon—that support sometimes looks like the universe yanking you outside just to remind you, you're still alive.

And sometimes it comes wrapped in fur.

Shelly's Shoes
When the Support You Need Shows Up Wearing Honesty.

My gallery was thriving.

A good portion of that success came from Shelly—my energetic framing guru, who could close a big art sale while holding a tape measure and a cup of coffee.

When she came to me, bursting with a "genius idea," I listened.

"Kate," she said, "West Michigan Furniture has a gallery space opening. What if we opened Moynihan North? You could still do the framing production downtown. It's perfect!"

The art showroom did make sense. So I signed the lease. Remodeled the space. Added inventory.

Days before opening? Shelly resigned.

She became a full-time independent designer—at West Michigan Furniture—meaning her focus was off art and on selling complete home ensembles.

My best salesperson. Gone. At the exact moment, the second store opened.

I wanted to breathe fire.

Three days later, my friend Mary came in.

After I unloaded every tangled feeling, she said six simple words: ""Kate, try seeing it from her side — walk a minute in Shelly's shoes."

And she laid out the truth gently:

Shelly's husband hated her weekend hours. The new job gave her freedom. She wasn't trying to hurt me. She was trying to save her marriage.

It didn't erase the sting. But it softened the hurt.

And that's support: someone who helps you hold a truth you wouldn't have reached alone.

The Christmas Tree Capers
*Support Sometimes Arrives with Branches,
Sky-blue paint, and Slippery Circumstances.*

Christmas inventory had arrived—sky-blue and red everything—the newest trend.

To showcase it in a gallery known for setting trends, I needed something bold.

The year before, I'd spray-painted a handful of six-foot, long-forgotten, needleless, Christmas trees white — recycling last season's dead ones into something unexpectedly elegant.

Bare branches. Soft light. Quietly gorgeous.

So this year, naturally, I needed to go bigger to illustrate the sky-blue trend.

Not taller-by-a-foot bigger.

Go-big-or-go-home bigger.

Thirteen feet. Multiple trees.

Bare branches reaching like question marks.

Painted sky-blue, of course.

And then placed dramatically throughout our 3,300-square-foot gallery.

There was only one problem: I lived above a downtown gallery surrounded by concrete. No 13-foot dead branches in sight.

Then my bonus daughter Allison spoke up: "My father-in-law has property up north. Acres of it. Want me to ask him?"

Yes. Please.

Soon we were hauling bundles of massive bare trees.

We laid them on a giant plastic tarp and fired up the paint sprayer. It took gallons of sky-blue paint, endless twisting and turning, and plenty of slipping. At one point, Larry skated across the tarp like an off-balanced penguin.

Once they were dry, we hauled them home, cementing large clusters into heavy pots, and spacing them throughout the gallery.

The result? Four towering sky-blue, 13-foot trees that stopped customers mid-stride.

The kind of display you can't buy—only build with help, humor, and people saying yes—and staying in the mess with you.

What Support Is Not

Sometimes the best support is knowing when *not* to ask for help.

My team members came with all kinds of strengths.

Jennifer's strength? Display magic.

Her ideas were dazzling—elaborate, playful, wildly ambitious.

And she'd sweep us into a project with enthusiasm: "We should build a full holiday mantle! And snowflakes! And twelve dangling garlands!"

And then, like clockwork...part-time Jennifer would leave for the day while the rest of us stayed behind to execute her masterpiece. Hours. Sometimes days.

Eventually, I learned to ask her one simple question: "Is this realistic?"

Jennifer would laugh and say, "My husband says the same thing about me at home. I'm the queen of the royal *we*—meaning *you*."

Support, I realized, isn't about saying yes to everything.

It's knowing which yes brings you life—and which one hands you a project you didn't sign up for.

Your Support
Already Around You

Support is not weakness. It's strength multiplied.

You are not meant to do life alone. No restart thrives in isolation.

Let people show up for you. Let yourself show up for them.

Because support isn't dependence. It's connection. And connection is what lets life expand you.

Chapter Twelve
The Right Person, Right Moment

Wisdom doesn't always arrive wrapped in formal lessons.

Sometimes it slips in sideways—disguised as a birder, a freckled stranger, or a moment you almost overlook.

If you're paying attention—even briefly—you catch something you didn't know you needed.

We talk a lot about lifelong mentors.

But we rarely talk about the blink-and-you-miss-them people— the ones who cross our path for a day, an hour, a sentence... and still leave a mark.

This chapter is for them.

Tails Up, Tails Down
How a Birder Taught Me to Stop Overthinking

Years ago in the gallery, I hung a small watercolor of three geese — each painted mid-glide, beaks angled slightly toward the center of the paper. To my eye, it created visual balance, a soft conversation happening midair.

A gentleman stopped in front of it, studied it, and tapped me on the shoulder. "Are those geese flying in or out?" he asked.

I must've looked puzzled.

He pointed. "If their tails are down, they're flying *in*. If their tails are up, they're flying *out*."

Ah — an avid birder.

I leaned in toward my own painting as if seeing it for the first time, squinting at three tiny, 3/8-inch geese. Their heads were stretched forward — not up, not down — so I took a gamble. "They're flying out," I said.

He nodded. "Good answer." And bought the painting.

I didn't think much of it then — just a funny moment between an artist and a man fluent in waterfowl body language.

But years later, his question keeps floating back to me.

Maybe that's the quiet truth of both art and life: We don't always know whether we're flying in or out. We just keep moving.

Maybe we don't need the whole map — just enough instinct to say, *It's time.*

Even if it feels early. Even if it feels late.

Even if we were perfectly comfortable on the pond yesterday.

So here's to moving like the geese: without overthinking, in good company, trusting the invisible currents that carry us forward.

How Pigtails Inspired Me
When Creativity Arrives on a Bicycle

We were camping that summer.

My sons biked endless loops around the dirt road, the air thick with sunscreen, sizzling burgers, and the stale scent of campfire smoke.

I sat at the picnic table, cutting strips from watercolor paintings gone wrong, hoping to salvage a collage.

My nine-year-old son Adam rode up.

Right behind him came a freckled-faced girl with braided pigtails and more confidence than both of us combined.

She winked at Adam and twirled a braid like she was starring in her own movie.

Adam cringed.

But both kids leaned over my scattered strips of paper, curiosity shining brighter than the campfire.

"I'm weaving them together," I explained.

"Like a hair braid," she said — still twirling.

It was a perfect idea.

Except my strips were too short.

"Use cattail reeds!" they sang in unison.

Before I could blink, Adam was back on his bike, pedaling double-time toward the frog pond. Between avoiding Freckles and gathering cattails, cattails won.

He returned holding an armful of reeds — and together we wove something beautiful.

All from a child I barely knew. A moment I never planned. And the spark for a new art piece.

Sometimes inspiration comes twirling a braid.

Sometimes it shows up on a bike.

Sometimes it's nine years old and has no idea it just changed your work forever.

Staying open-minded is a 10% shift.

Grandma Cake
Why Listening Matters More Than Being Right

My first grandchild, Jackson, was fourteen months old when I heard a strange sound.

We'd baked cookies earlier that day. Now he was propped in his booster seat at the table, eating dinner.

"Cake," he said.

I corrected him quickly. "No, we baked cookies. Not cake. You can have a cookie when your dinner is gone."

"Cake," he repeated.

I glanced at his mom, Allison.

She shrugged.

I tried again. "Jackson, you can have a cookie after dinner. We don't have any cake."

"Cake."

Back and forth we went until Allison laughed and said, "Kate… he's saying *your* name. He's trying to say *Kate*. Not cake."

And just like that, I learned two things:

- toddlers know what they mean even when we don't understand

- and sometimes we miss what's being said because we're too busy being right

From that day on, all of my grandkids have called me Grandma Cake.

Which feels about right —a reminder to listen more closely, assume less, and stay open to the sweetness trying to reach you.

A Farmer Shares a Wise Word
The Best Wisdom Often Comes with Feathers Attached

My sons and I were visiting a farm when Farmer Joe asked, "Want to fetch some eggs from the henhouse?"

We cheered, "Yes," imagining a charming little chore.

Twenty minutes later, we emerged with pecked hands, wild hair, and the distinct scent of *Eau de Chicken Barn* clinging to every fiber of our clothes.

Inside, Farmer Joe slipped on an apron and cracked eggs with the ease of someone who'd done it a million times.

I ducked into the bathroom to wash up.

When I came back, I nearly stepped on what looked like a glossy yellow eyeball.

An egg sat right on the floor.

Farmer Joe shrugged. "Must've flown out of the pan."

Then he chuckled and went right back to cooking — as if eggs frequently achieved escape velocity in his kitchen.

"It happens," he said. "What's done is done."

Something about that simple sentence stuck.

Because so often, we stand over our own messes — the dropped plans, the imperfect attempts, the things we wish we could redo — and shame ourselves.

Farmer Joe didn't. He just kept going. Sunny-side up.

The Shape of Brief Mentors and Moments

They come for a minute. They stay for a lifetime.

A stranger who buys your painting and gives you a metaphor.

A girl on a bike who twirls her hair and hands you a new idea.

A farmer who shrugs off a splattered egg.

We don't get to choose our brief mentors.

Or the brief moments.

But we do get to notice them.

It isn't how long we know someone that makes them memorable.

It's what we share with them.

And sometimes, one tiny exchange becomes a breadcrumb on the trail back to ourselves.

Chapter Thirteen
Break Mental Roadblocks

Why the stories we inherit shape what we believe—and how small shifts can rewrite the whole script

Some roadblocks are made of concrete.

Most, though?

They're made of stories. Old stories. Inherited stories. Half-true stories we swallowed whole without ever asking: *Is this even mine?*

Or did I just... absorb it?

Breaking mental roadblocks rarely requires a bulldozer.

Usually, it just takes a question. A pause. A slight tilt of the head.

A willingness to wonder: *What if this isn't the only way?*

The smelly shoes and an initiation drink that cracked my lens wide open.

The First Layer Is Allowed to Be Awkward

He asked me to go bowling. I haven't bowled in thirty years.

I knew in my gut this wasn't like riding a bike.

This required choosing the right ball weight, finding finger holes that fit, and somehow remembering the rhythm of swing and release.

Not to mention rented, slippery, smelly shoes.

I wanted to beg for the gutter guard.

But I needed to buck up.

I'd said yes to grandson, Liam's, bowling field trip—just like I'd said yes to starting a new painting series, *Restart Horizons*.

To do either, I had to dive in. And truthfully, diving in felt wobbly.

For the first time, I wasn't painting leaves and trees—my comfort zone.

Even my *Choose to Fly* birds had revolved around branches and bark.

Now I was letting the sky take over.

Big. Open. Unfamiliar.

Beginnings are always awkward. They ask you to commit before you feel ready. Every stroke feels like a question mark.

Too bold? Too soft? Too much?

But it's a start. And sometimes, that's enough.

The first layer won't stay visible for long.

It will be covered, shifted, built upon—but it's what makes everything else possible.

Was I the best bowler? No.

Did we laugh? Did I survive? Did I live life?

Yes. Yes. And yes.

That's how this new series feels too—uncertain, playful, and full of potential.

Because sometimes the only way forward is to pick up the ball, trust your swing, and let the sky lead the way.

Mental roadblocks often sound like:

This is how I've always done it.

This is my comfort zone.

This is my safe place.

But once you ask a single question—*Do I want more?* The story loosens its grip.

Think Beyond
The Mug that Saved My Mindset

In an online painting class, my instructor, Amanda challenged us to paint familiar subjects in unfamiliar ways. Looser. Tighter. Anything that disrupted habit.

I tried. Truly. All I got were muddy colors and rising frustration.

Sensing a meltdown, Amanda picked up a plain coffee mug and said, "Describe this ten different ways."

I started strong. A pencil holder. A paperweight. A planter.

Then the ideas slowed.

My brain stalled. I felt ridiculous.

"Keep going," she encouraged.

"A pudding dish. A brush-cleaning cup." Then… nothing.

She waited.

By the time I reached nine, the mug had become a bug house, a bird feeder, and a vessel I could shout my frustration into so my rant wouldn't break the sound barrier for the rest of the class.

Amanda smiled. "And ten?"

The only idea left was to hurl the mug onto the floor—shattering it into ceramic confetti.

Wait. That was the idea.

Smash it. Rebuild it. Turn it into a mosaic.

Suddenly, the exercise wasn't about mugs at all.

It was about the invisible fences in my thinking.

Mental roadblocks don't announce themselves.

They show up as exhaustion. Indecision.

The belief that there is only one right way.

Once you push past the first stuck place, possibilities multiply.

Rapid-Fire & Steady
Letting People Be Who They Are

My tween sons were creating chaos.

They were preparing Larry's *initiation drink*—their idea of welcoming him into the family after learning we were getting married.

Adam, eleven, led the mission. Into a pot went Gatorade, ketchup, green olives, a dollop of peanut butter, and—with flair—a handful of marshmallows.

Brian, twelve, hovered nearby, concern radiating off him like a smoke alarm.

When Adam cracked an egg into the mix, Brian couldn't stay silent. "You have to cook it," he insisted. "Or he'll get salmonella."

Adam turned up the stove, added hot sauce for good measure, and stirred.

By the time Larry arrived, a stench hovered in the kitchen.

"Drink up!" Adam cheered.

I watched in disbelief as Larry swallowed it.

"All of it?" I asked.

He shrugged. Then chuckled. "I have a cold. I can't taste a thing."

As the boys howled with laughter, something clicked.

Adam will always be rapid-fire—impulsive, imaginative, bold.

Brian will always be steady—thoughtful, cautious, deliberate.

Neither is wrong. Their differences weren't meant to be fixed. They were meant to be trusted.

Most of us lean naturally toward one rhythm—and then spend years shaming ourselves for not being the other.

One of the biggest mental roadblocks we inherit is the idea that there's only one correct way to be.

Pull the Trigger
Your Brain Loves Simple Reset Buttons

My friend Donna spent years teaching high-school English—a profession that deserves its own medal.

Between grading endless essays, decoding teenage body language, and keeping sixteen-year-olds awake during Shakespeare, her nervous system lived on high alert.

One afternoon, we sat down for tea. She poured two cups.

Peppermint steam curled upward, brushing my cheek.

My shoulders dropped a full inch.

She noticed. "It works every time," she said.

"What does?"

"This," she said, lifting her cup. "Peppermint tea is my reset trigger."

That scent was her restart button. A small act of self-command.

Since that afternoon, peppermint tea has become my trigger to reset too—not because it's magical, but because ritual tells your nervous system:

You can soften now.

You can exhale.

You can begin again.

Breaking a mental roadblock isn't always dramatic.

Sometimes it's a scent. A mug. A pause.

The Heart of This Chapter

Breaking mental roadblocks isn't about force.

It's about noticing. Questioning. Experimenting. Trying again.

Sometimes it looks like trusting awkward beginnings.

Sometimes it looks like smashing a mug—metaphorically or literally.

Sometimes it looks like honoring different rhythms in the same family.

Sometimes it looks like peppermint steam curling around your face.

But every time you challenge an inherited story, your world widens.

Every time you loosen a belief that no longer fits, you create space—like the negative space in a painting.

And every time you rewrite even a tiny part of your internal script, you authenticate a piece of yourself.

That—gently, steadily—is how a life transforms.

Chapter Fourteen
Be Open to New Opportunities

**Why the best moments
often come from accidental detours,
last-minute pivots, and plans that fall
apart in exactly the right way**

If life came with a GPS, most of us would use it religiously.

Clear routes. Predictable turns. Zero surprises.

But that's not how restarts work.

They show up disguised as inconveniences, mishaps, or flat-out disasters—and somehow become the moments that open doors we didn't even know were there.

Opportunity rarely knocks politely.

It shows up disguised as a ruined plan, a spicy mistake, or a dinner that goes hilariously wrong — and asks, "Now what?"

Too Hot to Handle
My Pepper Knowledge

A new bakery opened downtown, and the moment I stepped inside, I met destiny—

in the form of a decadent, glossy chocolate cake crowned with ruby-red candied rings.

It was love at first bite. Sweet. Velvety...and then a spicy kick.

"What on earth is this?" I asked.

"Serrano peppers," the baker said brightly.

Perfect, I thought.

Spicy cake for a gallery opening? Yes.

Even better—we could turn it into a game.

I pictured the sign immediately: **SERRANO PEPPER POWER** - Raw Pepper Eating Challenge. Winners featured on our Hall of Fame board.

I swung by the Mexican grocer, bought a dozen peppers, and spent the afternoon designing a poster board that practically radiated danger.

Enter Kim.

She studied the display, then asked the question that should have stopped me sooner: Kate... have you ever eaten a raw serrano pepper?"

I gave her a confident—meaning clueless—smile. "I've had bell peppers."

"Kaaaa-te," she said, stretching my name into a two-syllable warning. "Serranos are twice as hot as jalapeños. You can't feed these raw to customers. Someone might get sick."

My stomach dropped. My poster doomed. My ego wilted like overcooked spinach.

Time for Plan B. But what? This was last-minute.

The day happened to be unseasonably warm.

We pivoted. Hard. Whipping up lemonade and launching: **THE LEMON PUCKER POWER CHALLENGE.**

Customers lined up—grown adults—volunteering to suck on lemon wedges and try not to make the face. You know the one. The face that says, "Someone just told me my taxes are due today."

Eyes watered. Cheeks caved in. Shoulders shuddered.

We had more participants than any challenge we'd ever run.

The gallery roared with laughter.

Plan B didn't just save the day—it outshone Plan A in every possible way.

Sometimes opportunity arrives looking like a disaster…and ends up tasting like lemonade.

The Big Meltdown
Shifting Skis

My sons lived for skiing. So when Spring Break rolled around, we packed the van: Skis. Boots. Fleece. Enough snacks to feed a hockey team.

Warm front or not, the boys were convinced we'd find snow.

One hour north, Brian's phone pinged. Crystal Mountain: **CLOSED. No snow.**

Adam panicked. "Google Nubs Nob!"

Closed.

"Search Mount!"

"That's in Canada," I said gently. "Seven hours away. This is a two-day trip."

Silence. Heavy silence.

The kind that makes the air taste like disappointment.

Then—inspiration.

Or desperation. Hard to tell which.

"Try French Lick," I said.

The boys blinked. Googled. Screamed.

"GOLF! IT'S SEVENTY DEGREES! LET'S GO!"

We turned around. Stopped at home. Swapped skis for golf clubs.

And drove to Indiana for a sun-soaked adventure on the Pete Dye course.

Best Spring Break ever.

Born entirely from the trip that wasn't.

Sometimes opportunity hides under melted snow.

Things Aren't Always What They Appear
The Frigid Cookout With 'Heat'

Winter in North Dakota is an attitude test. Cold? Try *your-nose-may-actually-fall-off* cold.

But my sons loved grilled burgers, so one night I decided to be the brave, cool mom who grills in eight-degree weather.

Spoiler: Bravery is not always wisdom.

The charcoal wouldn't heat. The wind blew out every spark. The boys hovered, starving.

Finally, Brian said, "Marge keeps fire starters in the shed. Want me to grab some?"

Sure, I thought. Why not?

He returned with a handful of mysterious brown disks.

We tossed them in. INSTANT INFERNO.

Back in business.

Then our neighbor Bryce wandered over. "Whoa," he said. "You're grilling with cow pies."

"What?"

"Cow. Pies. Dried cow dung. Farmers use them as fuel."

My stomach dropped.

The burgers were discarded.

Dinner became hot dogs.

And honestly? It was perfect.

Because the burgers would've been forgotten.

But the cow-pie story? Legendary.

Sometimes opportunity comes disguised as embarrassment...and becomes the memory that lasts.

The Truth About New Opportunities

New opportunities rarely arrive neatly labeled.

They show up as:

- a ruined plan
- a closed ski resort
- a pepper hotter than your common sense
- a spark that won't light
- a dinner that goes hilariously wrong
- a moment that splits your path in two

They show up when we're not ready—but willing.

Opportunities don't ask for perfection.

They ask for openness. Curiosity. A willingness to pivot. To laugh. To try again.

Opportunity isn't about crafting a flawless plan.

It's about saying: "Well… that wasn't what I expected. Let's see what else is possible."

And that—right there—is where the magic sneaks in.

A 10% shift at exactly the right moment.

Chapter Fifteen
Follow Your Whispers

*Why the smallest signals often lead you
exactly where you need to go*

Most of us think "life direction" arrives with trumpets, clarity, or maybe an email subject line reading: **URGENT: HERE IS YOUR NEXT CALLING.**

But in truth? Life rarely shouts. It whispers.

Whispers are quiet nudges. Unexpected sparks.

A thought that returns more than once.

A tug under your ribs that says, *Maybe here. Maybe this.*

Joy showing up before you decide whether you're "ready" for it.

The problem is not that whispers aren't audible.

The problem is that we get too busy, too responsible, too grown-up to hear them.

Especially in midlife, when we've gotten very good at explaining ourselves out of what we want.

But whispers will wait.

And if you pay attention, they will reroute your life with the gentlest of hands.

Jude and the 6:15 a.m. Thud
Ready or Not

It was Saturday morning. Not my house. Too early for anyone to be awake.

And yet—a loud thud overhead.

My son was out of town, so I was staying overnight to care for the three grandkids. I bolted upstairs, prepared for every possibility except the one I found: My grandson Jude—fully dressed in his soccer uniform. Shin guards and all.

For a game more than six hours away.

"Why are you dressed already?" I whispered.

His answer bubbled out of him. "I can't wait. I'm playing center forward today," naming the most sought-after position on the team.

Joy was shooting straight out of him like confetti.

I wanted to send him back to bed.

I wanted my quiet morning.

My coffee. My sense of control.

But there it was—a whisper disguised as a wiggly eight-year-old in cleats.

Pay attention. This matters to him. Let delight go first.

So we moved through the morning differently.

Toast. Water bottle. Packing snacks.

His shin guards clacked against the stool as he tapped his foot— too excited to sit still.

That rhythmic tapping became a reminder:

Sometimes joy doesn't fit neatly into your schedule.

Sometimes it knocks on the ceiling and says, *Get up. There's something beautiful ahead.*

Whispers often start as excitement you didn't plan for.

That morning, Jude followed his joy.

And because he did—I followed mine.

Love Is...
The First Creative Whisper I Nearly Ignored

As a teenager, I loved the comic strip *Love Is...*—those simple little drawings with one-line truths. I'd read them in the *Detroit* newspaper, then started making my own.

Love is... your boyfriend patting the car seat, so you scoot closer.

Love is... your older boyfriend driving home from Michigan Tech just to take you to prom.

Silly. Sweet. Cheesy.

But something in me sparked every time. A flicker. A whisper.

Not of romance—but of creativity.

I'd sit with my pencil, doodling ideas, waiting for the next line to surface.

And it always did.

My mind would go quiet, and then a nudge would arrive: *Try this. Say it like that. What if...?*

But I didn't recognize it as creativity.

I thought I was just passing time.

Besides, I was convinced I'd become a homemaker like my mom— not someone whose life revolved around color and storytelling. Instead, I chose nursing because it felt dependable.

But the whisper was already there.

In doodles. In daydreams. In the way ideas came to me when I was still.

Whispers often begin long before we understand their purpose.

Love is...

The Substack Setup Saga
AKA: When a Whisper Won't Let Go

I have never claimed to be tech-savvy.

And after the day I had launching Substack—a story-based online space where I share personal essays—I never will.

The setup promised to take "30 minutes or less."

Four hours later, I was sweating, squinting, and second-guessing every button.

I wanted to quit at least seven times.

Then I remembered—I'd spent an hour designing the banner alone.

For that investment alone, I refused to give up.

Something was tugging at me—a whisper I didn't expect: *Keep going. You're supposed to share your stories here.*

So I kept clicking. Kept troubleshooting. Kept muttering dramatic accusations at my laptop.

And then—finally—it published.

Hours later, a notification popped up. My first subscriber comment. I nearly cried.

Not because of the tech victory—but because the whisper had been right.

This platform opened a new door for my voice, my art, my stories. And it only happened because I didn't silence the nudge telling me to try.

Whispers often sound like: *This matters. Don't walk away yet.*

Some whispers ask you to begin. Others ask you to keep going.

And sometimes—a whisper asks you to loosen a certainty you've been holding tight.

Sometimes a Whisper Makes You Change Your Mind

When I returned to college—leaving nursing behind and testing the waters of becoming a professional artist—I took nearly any art-related job I could find.

I taught an adult-ed watercolor class when I'd only taken one myself.

I slept on a cot at the local arts council, acting as the "cheap" overnight security system for a rare exhibition.

I weathered an art fair in Minneapolis, in 107-degree sweltering heat—proof that stubbornness sometimes counts as a skill.

If it paid and involved art, I said yes.

Except for one thing.

A local gallery showed my work and wanted me to sell framing. That meant measuring to the sixteenth of an inch—precision I had no patience for. I wanted to swing paint across a canvas, not fuss over corners.

I vowed that whatever I did, I would never own an art gallery.

Then I met Larry—a commercial photographer with a woodworking hobby and a mind that loved precision. When I landed a corporate commission for thirty-two paintings that required custom wood frames, he volunteered to help.

We worked beautifully together.

When we decided to move back to Michigan as a married couple, reality arrived quickly. Digital photography was emerging, and Larry's profession was at a crossroads: invest heavily or change direction. We didn't have the money to invest.

Our minds spun.

"Let's do retail," Larry said one day. "Open an art gallery. I could be the framer."

I raised an eyebrow.

Not because it was a bad idea—but because it challenged a story I'd told myself for years: That I'd never own an art gallery.

My dream of moving back to Michigan—to be closer to my family—was suddenly within reach. All it required was swallowing my pride and admitting I might do the very thing I'd sworn I wouldn't.

We found a long, narrow storefront in downtown Holland. In 1993, it was a town with more potential than polish.

As I signed the lease, the pen slick in my hand, a question pulsed through me: *Could we really sell enough art to cover this rent?*

I told my self-doubt to scram and silently repeated, *We have a plan.*

The plan was simple: if the gallery struggled, we'd build a movable wall.

The front half would be my art.

The back would become Larry's photography studio—old equipment and all.

We'd roll the wall toward whichever business needed more space.

It wasn't a guarantee. It was a willingness. It was flexible thinking.

The art business prospered, and we never built the wall. It was a delightful 25-year run.

But that's not the point of this story.

The point is this:

Sometimes a whisper doesn't ask you to begin something new.

Sometimes it asks you to release an old certainty.

To change your mind.

To go in a direction you once promised yourself you never would.

The Truth About Following Whispers

Whispers aren't logical.

They don't present spreadsheets. They don't ask your permission.

They show up as:

- curiosity
- anticipation
- creativity tapping its foot
- the sense that something is growing inside you
- an urge to try something unfamiliar or something you said you'd never do
- winning when you're completely out of your comfort zone

Whispers don't insist. They invite. They don't push. They pull.

And the more you listen—the more your life begins to align with the truest parts of you.

Your Whispers
Already Here

Sit quietly for a moment. Notice the flickers.

What's tugging at your attention?

What's lighting up your imagination?

What's waking you earlier than usual?

What's returning, again and again, asking to be heard?

Those aren't accidents. They're invitations. Follow them.

They won't always lead you where you expected.

They may lead you somewhere earlier, quieter, or more inconvenient than planned.

But they will take you someplace honest.

Maybe even someplace you never imagined—like an unexpected thump above your head at 6 a.m., leading you upstairs to a soccer-ready grandson and a day quietly asking you to show up.

Chapter Sixteen
Decide, Then Ask for Support Not Permission

How courage grows when you finally choose yourself

During a painful season, a wise counselor gave me one simple instruction.

"I want you to journal every day," she said. "But don't look back for three weeks."

"Why?" I whispered. My throat felt tight—like I was swallowing tears before they could spill.

"It's nearly impossible to see change from one day to the next," she explained. "But when you look back later, you'll see the shift. And that's what reassures you."

I wasn't convinced. But I wrote anyway.

Night after night. Page after page. Tears soaking the paper.

And I didn't look back.

Slowly, the tears softened. Then stopped.

Some nights, I didn't even reach for the notebook.

Something was changing—quietly, subtly—long before I could name it.

Then one day, I realized something had shifted.

The voice that used to scold me like a child had begun to lose its grip.

The sharp *shoulds*. The second-guessing.

The running commentary about what I was doing wrong.

They grew quieter as I grew steadier.

Shame loosened. Guilt thinned. Old accusations evaporated.

Kinder words took their place.

Little by little, courage returned.

And with it—hope.

So I made a decision.

I forgave the younger version of myself who believed following someone else would lead to happiness.

I treated myself with the same tenderness I had always offered my children.

And when I did? Momentum gathered.

Not because someone gave me permission.

But because I finally chose to give it to myself.

I never looked back at that tear-stained journal. I didn't need to.

When Fear Shows Up First

Years earlier, I had moved—again—and found myself once more as the new nurse.

Low seniority. Rotating shifts. The dreaded night shift—my personal nightmare.

At the same time, I stumbled into a watercolor class that lit something up in me.

Remember my mention of *Love Is…* cartoons as a teen—simple sketches that expressed what I couldn't yet say out loud? They stumbled into my mind too.

With the little watercolor knowledge I had, a passion for my earlier *Love Is* cartoon figure, and the news that the local hospital was remodeling the pediatric wing—an idea arrived. A big one:

A children's hospital mascot.

A coloring book to comfort young patients.

A badge system so kids could earn "Bravery Badges."

A parent newsletter.

Wallpaper borders.

A painting for every pediatric room.

I assembled it all into a portfolio and asked for a meeting.

The only person willing to see me? The facilities manager. (Also known as the furnace guy.)

Fear growled in my chest, telling me not to bother. But I kept the appointment. It turned out he knew the VP.

Within minutes, I went from standing in front of a man holding a wrench to presenting in the CEO's office.

I got the job. All of it.

That work gave me income. And confidence. And proof.

Enough to return to college.

Enough to major in art.

Enough steadiness to tell my mother.

Enough to become Kate.

I've been a full-time artist ever since.

That's what happens when you stop waiting for permission—and decide to believe in yourself first.

When Fear Comes Back (Because It Will)

Years later, fear tried again.

I'd been painting watercolors for eleven years—loving their softness, their unpredictability.

Then 9/11 happened. The recession followed. The gallery went quiet.

I needed something bold. Alive. Something that could pull people back in.

So I dragged out my old oil paints.

Bought my first large canvas.

Placed it in the front window—on full display—as if confidence were already mine.

It wasn't.

I felt rusty. Intimidated. Utterly unsure.

But I painted anyway.

The first layers were muddy. The second was worse. Still, I kept going.

I switched from wide brushes to tiny ones. From thin paint to thick.

And then—frustrated and surrendered—I picked up a palette knife.

It felt like meeting an old friend I didn't know I'd been missing.

Color moved. Edges softened. Something clicked.

People didn't just buy the work—they connected with it.

They saw something honest. Alive. Unapologetic.

That connection carried me forward.

Not because fear disappeared.

But because I decided and stayed true to myself.

When Courage, Not Fear, Is the Decision

More recently, courage showed up as something much smaller.

I dropped off new paintings at Lake Effect Gallery—the downtown gallery hosting some of my work.

Inside, I noticed a couple quietly studying my art.

Out of a gallery full of local artists, they had landed on mine.

A tingle moved through me.

Was it fear—or excitement?

I've learned it's not always easy to tell the difference.

A familiar voice chimed in, questioning why I thought I was good enough to approach two strangers—especially when it wasn't my gallery.

But this time, I didn't let it drive.

I chose a different voice. *Go for it, Kate.*

Smiling, I introduced myself.

They were visiting from Cincinnati—five hours away—and dressed like a coordinated travel ad: one in black, one in white.

They mentioned they were looking for a specific size, so I asked Amy, the gallery assistant, to show them a few more pieces down-stairs. (It still didn't feel like my place to escort them.)

I headed to the framing area, chatted with Deb about prices, and turned to leave.

When I came back up front, my Cincinnati couple was still there—still dressed in black and white—still gazing at my paintings.

Amy was nowhere in sight.

So I asked if they had any more questions.

They blinked. "No one's spoken to us yet."

Wait. What? Had I entered a paint-fume déjà vu?

Just then, the basement door swung open—and up came *another* couple—dressed in black and white. And from Cincinnati.

There we stood, all five of us, laughing at the perfect copy-and-paste moment life had just pulled off. (Even better? They lived in neighboring districts back home and had never met.)

Each couple fell in love with a different painting and took one home.

Coincidence? Connection?

Either way, I'll take it as a reminder: Art does its work when we're willing to show up. Confident in ourselves. Confident in our decisions.

The Heart of It

Every meaningful change begins the same way: With a decision.

Not a guarantee. Not approval. Not certainty.

A choice. Decide who you want to be.

Then ask for support—not permission.

Because permission keeps you waiting.

Decisions keep you moving.

And every brave step begins with this quiet truth: **Today, you are deciding to choose yourself.**

Chapter Seventeen
Live with Heart and Self-Compassion

Because gentleness toward yourself is strength, not softness

Some lessons arrive in grand moments.

Others slip in quietly—tucked into a borrowed pair of shoes, a child's trembling goodbye, a frozen lake, or a single winter branch someone thought to send you.

Self-compassion rarely announces itself.

It arrives as a nudge. A pause.

A small opening in the middle of an ordinary day that asks, gently: *What if you treated yourself with the same kindness you offer everyone else?*

These are the moments that taught me how.

The Wingtips in Atlanta
Letting Others Carry You When You Forget the Basics

Every January, Allison and I traveled to the Atlanta Gift Market—a five-day marathon inside twenty-five floors of wholesale showrooms.

We scouted trends. Placed orders. Walked miles.

It was our bi-annual ritual of inspiration and exhaustion.

The night before our flight, a storm rolled in, so Allison and I stayed at my son's house near the airport.

At 4 a.m., bleary-eyed and half awake, I reached into my suitcase and realized: I only had my snow boots.

No shoes. Not one pair.

And we were about to walk miles of showrooms—in a fashion-forward industry—with Allison, who somehow always looks like she stepped out of a boutique catalog.

My son's shoes were too big. My petite daughter-in-law's were too small.

But too big was better than heavy insulated boots.

So I laced up a pair of men's brown wingtips. Stiff. Heavy. Ridiculous.

And Allison—bless her—didn't laugh. She didn't even flinch.

She simply adjusted her pace and walked beside me, as if clunky men's shoes were a perfectly reasonable choice for a buying trip.

Sometimes, self-compassion is letting others support you.

Sometimes, it's allowing laughter to soften embarrassment.

And sometimes, it's walking twenty-five floors in borrowed wingtips and realizing that love often looks like steady company.

What Blooms Even in February
Aunt Ruth's Lesson in Tending Small Joys

Some acts of compassion arrive quietly.

Larry's Aunt Ruth was eighty-six the winter she taught me what tenderness looks like in a hard season.

It was February in Iowa—the brittle cold where sound seems to freeze midair.

Ruth stepped outside anyway.

Wrapped in an old coat that smelled faintly of lavender, she crunched across her frosted yard and clipped a handful of branches from her dormant pussy willow bush.

Thin. Closed. Unremarkable.

Then she mailed them to me.

When the box arrived days later, I was confused. Bare twigs. No explanation.

But when I placed them in a jar of water, something shifted.

Slowly. Tenderly.

Each bud softened. Unfurled. Then burst into small puffs of white.

In the middle of February—a quiet bloom.

At the time, I thought it was just Ruth being Ruth. Sweet. Quirky. Thoughtful.

Now I understand.

She wasn't sending branches. She was sending permission.

Permission to soften.

Permission to trust small shifts.

Permission to let gentle things matter.

Ruth didn't bulldoze through winter. She coaxed something alive—and shared it.

You don't need a whole garden to feel supported. One softened bud is enough.

And this, too: I didn't know Ruth long before she passed.

But relationships aren't measured in time. They're measured in what's shared.

Ruth shared a winter branch and taught me how to bloom again.

The Hand-on-Heart Goodbye
Where Tenderness Becomes Compassion

Goodbyes were always hard for my older son, Brian.

He's my deep-feeling one—thoughtful, sensitive, earnest.

As a child, parting overwhelmed him.

So we created a ritual.

Before saying goodbye, I'd guide his small hand to his chest, then place mine on top.

"Do you know what love is?" I'd ask.

He'd look up, listening.

"It's being able to feel joy—birthdays, ice-cream days, the moment school lets out. But to feel joy, you also have to feel the opposite. That's what goodbye is—the part that reminds you your heart works."

Then we'd hug — or maybe more accurately, I hugged him.

Brian was careful, reserved even then.

But I leaned in close enough to feel his breath steady beneath my hand.

It was compassion in practice.

Because teaching our children how to soften through sadness teaches us the same.

Self-compassion isn't avoiding emotion.

It's letting your heart feel—without apology.

The Year of Black Beauty
Finding Warmth in the Mess We Didn't Plan

I grew up with a holiday warning slightly different from most families.

While Ralphie's mom in *A Christmas Story* was worried about BB guns and eyesight, my mom had one repeating December refrain:

"Don't knock over the Christmas tree!"

My older brother Gregg and I, of course, managed to knock it over anyway. More than once. And mostly me—the spitfire gal.

But the year that lives forever in my memory is 1960—the year of Black Beauty.

Every December, Mom bundled Gregg and me into our snowsuits and drove from our home in Redford to Hudson's Department

Store in downtown Detroit—the tall one on Woodward Avenue that made you tilt your head all the way back just to see the top.

The moment we stepped onto the sidewalk, the world felt bigger.

The wind felt colder.

And we felt smaller—but in the very best way.

Forty-nine elaborate Christmas windows twinkled with animated elves, reindeer, and toys that seemed to leap to life behind the glass. My heart thump-thumped just knowing what waited inside.

We stepped through the doors into warm air and the smell of fresh sugar cookies—the same ones Mom baked every December. Then came the shuffle through the crowd toward one of the fifty-one elevators. When the doors opened and the uniformed attendant asked, "Which floor?" our bouncing boots practically yelled, **"Twelve!"**

That was where the North Pole lived.

Snow-dusted trees lined the aisles. Elves hammered and sawed away at toys. And somewhere in the middle of it all, Santa waited for us with a velvet lap and a laugh that made the whole floor vibrate.

But Santa wasn't the only mission.

Every year, Mom let us choose one ornament. Any ornament.

It was magical.

I always picked a plush animal—usually something soft enough to tuck into my mittened hand.

But that year, Gregg reached for…a giant jet-black glass globe.

"The black one?" Mom asked, trying to keep her voice from cracking.

Gregg nodded fiercely. A grin spread across his nine-year-old face.

Back home, he hung **Black Beauty**—now formally named—front and center.

And the next morning, determined to find a "better spot," he plucked it from the tree just as our dog, Zorro, barreled through my legs. My arms pinwheeled, taking Black Beauty—and the tree—with me.

You can imagine the rest.

Tree, brother, ornaments, and the beloved Black Beauty hit the floor in a single spectacular crash. Water from the stand soaked the carpet. Shards glittered everywhere like tragic little diamonds.

Mom froze.

Gregg whimpered.

And I—ever the helper—said, "It's okay, we'll clean it up."

And we did.

Now, years later, I'm convinced the real problem was the too-small tree stand Dad insisted on using. (I have since inherited his non-mechanical gene.)

But here's what stays with me now that I'm grown:

That tippy tree.

The broken ornaments.

The mess.

The togetherness.

It is all part of the warmth I feel every December.

Because those imperfect, chaotic moments became the stories we tell—the ones that crack us up, soften us, and remind us how much love is in the room even when the tree was sideways.

And tucked inside those memories is a kind of gratitude that sneaks up on you.

The messy kind.

The human kind.

The kind that **lets** you know you are loved. You are together—even when the tree topples over.

The Heart of This Chapter

Living with self-compassion isn't about self-pampering.

It's about permission.

Permission to be human.

Permission to be held.

Permission to soften instead of soldier through.

Permission to bloom in February.

Permission to laugh in borrowed shoes.

Permission to place a hand on your heart and remember that joy and sorrow are stitched from the same cloth.

Self-compassion is not weakness. It's a recalibration. A 10% shift. A way of choosing gentleness so your heart can stay open for what comes next.

And here is the quiet truth I want you to carry forward: **Self-compassion is how courage sustains itself.**

Kindness toward yourself is how you remain brave enough to love well—and live fully.

PART V

LIVING THE RESTART LIFE

One 10% Shift at a Time

Chapter Eighteen
A Gentle Beginning

Magic has a funny way of revealing itself.

I don't mean magic as something mystical or distant. I mean the quiet alignment of timing, people, and courage — and our intuition that nudges us forward — the moments that feel like coincidence until you look back and see a thread running through them.

Not all at once. Not in glittering fireworks or grand epiphanies.

More often, it arrives quietly—as a nudge you almost ignore, an unexpected offer, a coincidence that feels just a little too precise to dismiss.

And when you're living a shifted life, you begin to notice something important: Magic isn't rare. It's rhythmic.

It taps the side of your life gently and says, *This way... look here... try that... keep going*.

The trick isn't to chase it. It's to receive it. To grow it.

And growing magic—much like growing confidence, resilience, or courage—happens the same way everything in this book has unfolded: A little at a time.

Serendipity in Motion
When magic hides inside what almost breaks you

I met my future husband while crawling across an eight-foot painted backdrop.

Not exactly the kind of meet-cute you see in movies.

At the time, Larry was simply a photographer I had hired—not yet the man who would later help me rebuild a life.

But now, looking back, it feels perfectly on-brand for the life I was building: creative, messy, hopeful, and quietly stubborn.

I hired Larry—then a commercial photographer—to shoot professional images of my watercolor paintings. He noticed the texture immediately and asked a simple question.

"How big can you paint?"

Before I knew it, we were planning a VHS how-to video for photographers.

(Yes, VHS. Peak 1990. Pre-YouTube. Pre-everything.)

The idea was simple.

I'd paint giant eight-foot paper backdrops on camera, demonstrating how photographers could create their own custom portrait backgrounds.

He handled the lights and cameras.

I supplied the paint and the elbow grease.

It was fun. Exhausting. And it left my clothes with more splatters than any reasonable person would consider acceptable.

Quietly, I hoped the project would become my *Moving Back to Michigan* money—the savings I needed to return home.

It didn't.

The tapes barely sold.

But something else was happening—something softer, quieter, impossible to measure at the time.

We enjoyed working side by side.

We trusted each other's instincts.

We made something together.

That, as it turned out, was the beginning of the real magic.

Not long after—while I was still trying to make sense of what had *worked* and what hadn't—life intervened in its own unmistakable way.

I had just set up for a local Bismarck outdoor art fair when the sky opened.

A downpour flattened my booth.

Paintings drenched. Hair plastered. Shoes sloshing.

Total disaster.

A man walked up through the rain and handed me his business card.

I stood there dripping and defeated, assuming it was a polite gesture offered out of pity.

On Monday, I called.

He ordered thirty-two large original paintings for U.S. Healthcare's corporate offices.

(Yes, the same thirty-two I mentioned earlier.)

Enough to finally move back to Michigan.

Enough to restart my life.

By then, my friendship with Larry had deepened. His woodworking hobby became the perfect solution for the frames I suddenly needed in bulk. And we found ourselves working side by side again.

Synchronicity? Definitely.

And when he eventually proposed? Double serendipity.

Looking back, I can see it clearly now: Magic didn't arrive in the VHS tape we poured ourselves into.

It arrived in the wet, ruined art fair I thought had broken me.

It arrived disguised as failure.

Magic often does.

Magic Isn't Luck — It's Cultivation

If you look at your own life—honestly—you may see the same pattern.

Moments that felt random.

Doors that closed just in time to redirect you.

People who appeared exactly when you needed them.

Disappointments that later revealed themselves as turning points.

Magic rarely feels magical in the moment.

It feels like:

- interruption
- inconvenience
- coincidence
- discomfort
- something small and easy to overlook

But over time, you notice the truth: Magic grows when you are open to growth—even just a bit.

It shows up for the person willing to stay curious.

To shift gently instead of forcefully.

To begin before certainty arrives.

To trust the next small nudge.

Magic has never been missing from your life.

You've just been learning how to recognize it.

Your Magic (Already Growing)

You don't need a perfect business plan.

You don't need a five-step system.

You don't need to know the entire path.

You only need to notice what's already stirring:

- the curiosity that won't leave you alone
- the idea that keeps circling back
- the color you're drawn to
- the conversation that lifts you
- the longing you can't quite explain
- the quiet inner push to try
- the gentle tug toward begin

Magic isn't something you earn.

It's something you notice.

And when you notice it—you grow it.

So take one step toward what lights you. Just one.

A 10% shift.

A small, brave move.

A simple, *let's see where this goes.*

Because here's the truth that holds this entire book together: Most of the work is deciding.

The rest is showing up—gently, imperfectly, and with heart—for what's already unfolding inside you.

And then? You let life meet you there.

A Gentle Reminder

You don't need to restart your life all at once.

You already know how to live this way now.

One breath. One noticing. One choice. One small shift at a time.

The magic was never out there.

It's been growing inside you all along.

And it's ready when you are.

FINAL REFLECTIONS

Grow the Magic That's Already Inside You
An invitation to live the restart, one gentle shift at a time

By now, you've met the cast of characters who shaped me—

my sons who kept me on my toes,

the women who caught me when I fell,

the customers who surprised me,

the brave little moments that cracked me open.

But beneath all those stories is something quieter: a woman slowly becoming herself.

And to understand that, you have to know about my name.

I began as **Kathleen**—a name that sounded beautiful in other people's mouths but felt one size too big on me. Soft. Lyrical. A lullaby sort of name.

I never felt quite worthy of it.

Like wearing a dress with too much fabric and not enough courage.

Then came kindergarten.

My teacher asked, "Do they call you Kathy?"

Something in me clicked. Shorter. Lighter. A little more spunk.

A name I could grow inside of.

So I said yes.

And Kathy carried me through a lot—early love, heartbreak, a misguided move a thousand miles from home, and more than a few seasons where I believed happiness was something someone else could hand me.

It took me until midlife to realize what I had been teaching my own sons all along:

you can't feel joy without knowing sadness.

And you can't become yourself while holding someone else's map. No matter how well-intentioned, it will always lead you somewhere other than home.

When I finally understood that—truly understood it—I shed Kathy like a snakeskin.

I became **Kate**.

Not because the world changed.

But because I did.

Kate is the woman who trusts her timing.

Who listens, more than she apologizes.

Who notices, the small joys—

a grandson's early-morning thud on the ceiling,

a tulip painting gone wrong turned into something right,

a pussy willow bud blooming in February.

Kate is the version of me who follows the whispers instead of the worry.

And just when I thought I understood that lesson, life offered one more quiet reminder—this time in real time.

That moment reminded me of something this book has been quietly teaching all along: meaningful change rarely arrives as a grand announcement—it comes through small yeses we almost dismiss.

Last October, signs of Christmas were everywhere—grocery aisles, ads I swear I never searched for, and my grandchildren's notoriously long wish lists.

After years of fourth-quarter gallery sales, I understood what people were really looking for during the holidays: something meaningful. Something that felt personal. Something that carries a message.

Since retiring, I'd tried creating small gift items—ornaments, journals, candles. Each idea sold a little, then fizzled. No reorders. No spark.

Then one afternoon, I came across a batch of plain paper-mâché angels.

My practical voice said, *No. You've tried this before.*

But a quieter one asked, *What if?*

Days later, I ordered a dozen. I told myself they'd make nice gifts if nothing else.

They sold within minutes.

When I went to reorder, the blanks were sold out for the season.

That's when Larry stepped in—twirling one of the painted angels in his hand.

"I think I can make these," he said, already thinking in measurements and solutions as his 3D printer came to mind.

He did.

And suddenly, angels were traveling places I hadn't planned for—

to an isolated mother when her daughter couldn't be there,

to siblings grieving a grandmother they called Moma Love Dove,

to homes that needed comfort more than decoration.

Nothing about it was dramatic.

But it mattered.

Restarts don't knock—they tap, patiently, until we're willing to answer.

And here's the truth I want to hand you, gently and clearly: you don't have to change your whole life to feel different inside it.

You only need a small shift.

Just enough to interrupt old patterns.

Just enough to loosen what no longer fits.

Just enough to remind your heart it's still beating, still curious, still capable of wonder.

Everything you need is already inside you—

your magic,

your courage,

your creativity,

your softness,

your authenticity,

your restart.

It's been there since the beginning.

This book isn't the story of a woman reinventing herself from scratch.

It's the story of a woman finally becoming who she was always meant to be.

And now—it's your turn.

Not to leap.

Not to overhaul.

Not to chase someone else's idea of a life.

Just to shift. Gently. Steadily. Kindly.

Begin where you are.

Let the next right thing be small.

Let your courage come in the size that fits you.

Let your heart be the compass.

And when the whispers come—those tiny nudges, the quiet yeses, the ideas that won't leave you alone—please listen.

They're trying to guide you home to the most true, most tender, most beautifully *you* version of yourself.

I'll be right here cheering you on.

Begin again, friend.

Your restart is waiting.

Nothing is late. Nothing is wasted.

You are exactly where your next small shift can begin.

Acknowledgements

This book is about small shifts — quiet decisions, gentle courage, and the ways a life changes not all at once, but over time.

But no shift happens in isolation.

None of this exists without the people who live inside these pages every day: my sons, Brian and Adam, my daughter-in-law, Carrie, and my bonus daughter, Allison, as well as my grandchildren and friends who continue to teach me more than they realize — often without knowing they're teaching at all. Their presence, questions, humor, and patience have shaped how I see the world and how I move through it.

My deepest gratitude goes to my husband, Larry — my partner in life, art, and a thousand quiet acts of belief. He has stood beside me through uncertainty, reinvention, and more creative messes than either of us could have predicted. His steadiness made this work possible.

And my mom.

She has now passed, but her presence — in all its complexity — shaped the woman behind this book. She shaped the woman behind these pages — through love, through expectation, through tension, and through the unspoken lessons that take a lifetime to understand. Our relationship was not simple, but it was formative. And I carry it with me still.

This book may be about small shifts, but it stands on deep support.

I thank them for walking with me — then and now.

A Book Club Conversation Guide

This book wasn't written to be studied.

It was written to be shared.

If you're reading The 10% Shift with others, consider these questions as gentle starting points—not an agenda. You don't need to answer them all. You don't even need to answer them in order.

Let the conversation wander.

Let laughter show up where it wants to.

And if someone needs to pause for a refill, a stretch, or a deep breath—consider that part of the process.

Conversation Starters

1. Where did you feel most seen while reading this book?
(The moment that made you think, Oh. Me too.)

2. Was there a story or idea that stayed with you longer than you expected?
What do you think it was asking you to notice?

3. How do you personally recognize when you're in a "restart" season?
Is it loud and obvious—or quiet and sneaky?

4. The book suggests that small shifts can be powerful.

What does a "10% shift" look like in your life right now—something doable, not dramatic?

5. Which idea in the book felt comforting?
Which one felt a little uncomfortable (in the "hmm… that might be true" way)?

6. How do you usually respond when life feels uncertain?
Do you rush, freeze, overthink—or head for the metaphorical bathtub and ice cream?

7. What does resilience mean to you now—and how is that different from how you once defined it?

8. The book talks about emotional weather.
What kind of weather season do you feel like you're in right now?

9. Where do you feel pressure to have things "figured out"?
What would change if you gave yourself permission to move more slowly?

10. What practices—or people—help you return to yourself when things feel off balance?

11. Was there anything you disagreed with, questioned, or resisted while reading?
(Those moments often lead to the best conversations.)

12. As you finish this book, what's one small shift you feel curious about—not committed to, just curious?

A final note for your group

There's no right way to have this conversation.

Some insights arrive through words.

Some arrive through laughter.

Some arrive on the drive home.

And some arrive later—when you least expect them.

That counts too.

www.ingramcontent.com/pod-product-compliance
Lightning Source LLC
Chambersburg PA
CBHW040756120726
48005CB00012B/1205